UNVEILED

Overcoming Trauma to Walk in Your Divine Purpose

Women's Stories of Resilience and Healing

SHENITA V. BOLTON, Ed.S.

HOV
PUBLISHING

UNVEILED
Overcoming Trauma to Walk in Your Divine Purpose
Women's Stories of Resilience and Healing

Unless otherwise noted, Scriptures are taken from The King James Bible Online https://www.kingjamesbibleonline.org/. Copyright © 2025 King James Bible Online™ Used by permission. All rights reserved.

The Holy Bible: New King James version. Copyright © 2009 Thomas Nelson Inc. (Original work published 1982).

HOV Publishing a division of HOV, LLC.
www.hovpub.com
hopeofvision@gmail.com

Front Cover Design by Hope of Vision Designs
Cover and Interior Image Credits: Kasper Ravlo, Versusstudio
Inside layout by Hope of Vision Designs
Editor/Proofread: HOV Publishing Editorial Team

Contact the Author, Shenita V. Bolton, Ed.S.
shenitavbolton@gmail.com

For further information regarding special discounts on bulk purchases, please contact shenitavbolton@gmail.com.

ISBN Paperback: 978-1-955107-15-0
ISBN eBook: 978-1-955107-14-3

A SPECIAL DEDICATION

A Special Dedication to My Third Grade Teacher,
Louise Whitaker

In a classroom filled with wonder and light,
Stood Mrs. Whitaker, a beacon shining bright.
With a heart so kind and eyes that could see,
She believed in a little Black child, she believed in me.

In the third grade, I was young and unsure,
But Mrs. Whitaker's belief was my cure.
She saw potential where others saw none,
And whispered words of encouragement, one by one.

"You can do it Shenita," she said with a smile so true,
"Believe in yourself, there's nothing you can't do."
Her words were like magic, they lifted me high,
And sparked a flame that would never die.

Through challenges and triumphs, she stood by my side,
Guiding me with wisdom, filling me with pride.
She spoke life into me, she planted a seed,
That grew into a dream, a vision I would heed.

Now at 56 years old, I look back with gratitude,
For the mentor, the teacher, whose love renewed.
Mrs. Whitaker, you will forever hold a place in my heart,
For believing in a little Black girl and playing a vital part.

Your legacy lives in all that I do,
For now I am an educator just like you.
Thank you, dear teacher, for shaping my past,

For all your guidance, my future was cast.

THANK YOU, MRS. WHITAKER

ACKNOWLEDGEMENTS

This project could not have been completed without the help of God and the amazing women who opened their hearts and souls, sharing their raw, unfiltered stories with me and making this book a reality.

A special thanks to my husband, Brian Bolton: your unwavering support, love, and understanding made this journey possible. Thank you for being my constant. To my daughter, Chaslyn Piper: your presence and words of encouragement light up my life every day. To my bonus daughters, Brianna Bolton, Latrice Bolton, and Patricia Miles: thank you for your endless love and for welcoming me into your lives.

I am deeply grateful for my five grandchildren, who are a great source of inspiration and who remind me daily to be the best version of "MiMi" that I can be. To my parents, siblings, extended family, church family, closest friends, my sisters of Alpha Kappa Alpha Sorority, Incorporated, and my colleagues: thank you for your continuous support and belief in me.

This book stands as a testament to the power of vulnerability and the strength found in sharing our stories. To each and every one of you, thank you for being part of this incredible journey.

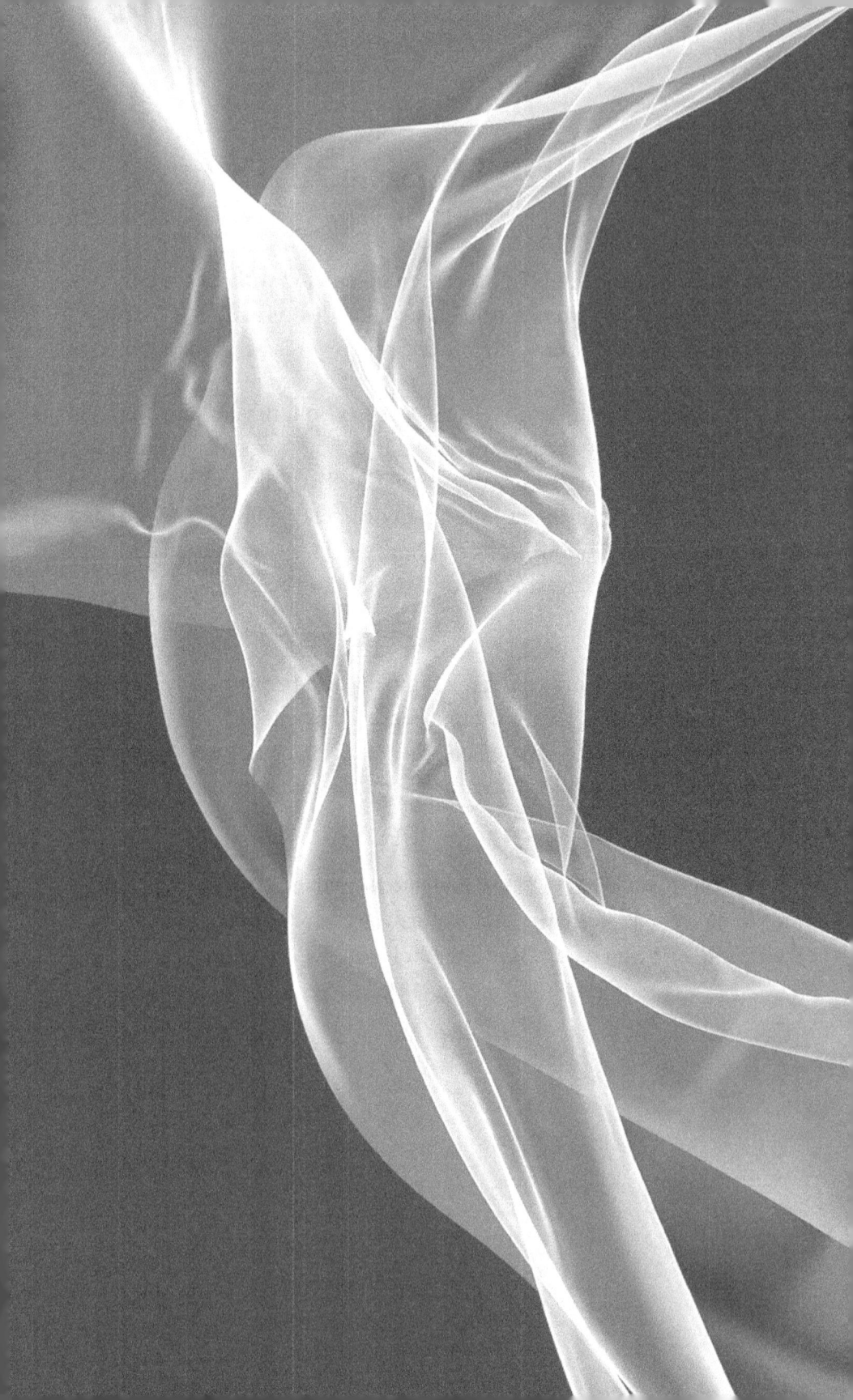

CONTENTS

PREFACE

In a world where challenges often overshadow our potential, the journey of healing and self-discovery can feel overwhelming. *Unveiled: Overcoming Trauma to Walk in Your Divine Purpose* is more than a book; it's a beacon of hope for women weighed down by past hurts, pains, and experiences, yet yearning for a brighter, purposeful future.

Trauma can manifest and shape our perceptions, relationships, and aspirations in countless ways, yet within each of us lies an innate resilience and a divine purpose waiting to be revealed. This book is a testament to faith and the transformative power of breaking free from the chains of past trauma.

Within these pages, you will discover a blend of personal stories, scriptures, and spiritual wisdom, designed to guide you on your own journey. Each chapter serves as a testament and a stepping stone, encouraging you to confront your past, embrace your authentic self, and step boldly into your unique purpose.

As you embark on this journey of transformation, remember—you are not alone. Many women have walked this path before you, and countless others stand ready to support you. Let *Unveiled* inspire you to reclaim your narrative, heal your wounds, and walk confidently in your divine purpose. You matter, and your story matters. The world is waiting for you to share it.

Welcome to your journey of unveiling the extraordinary within you.

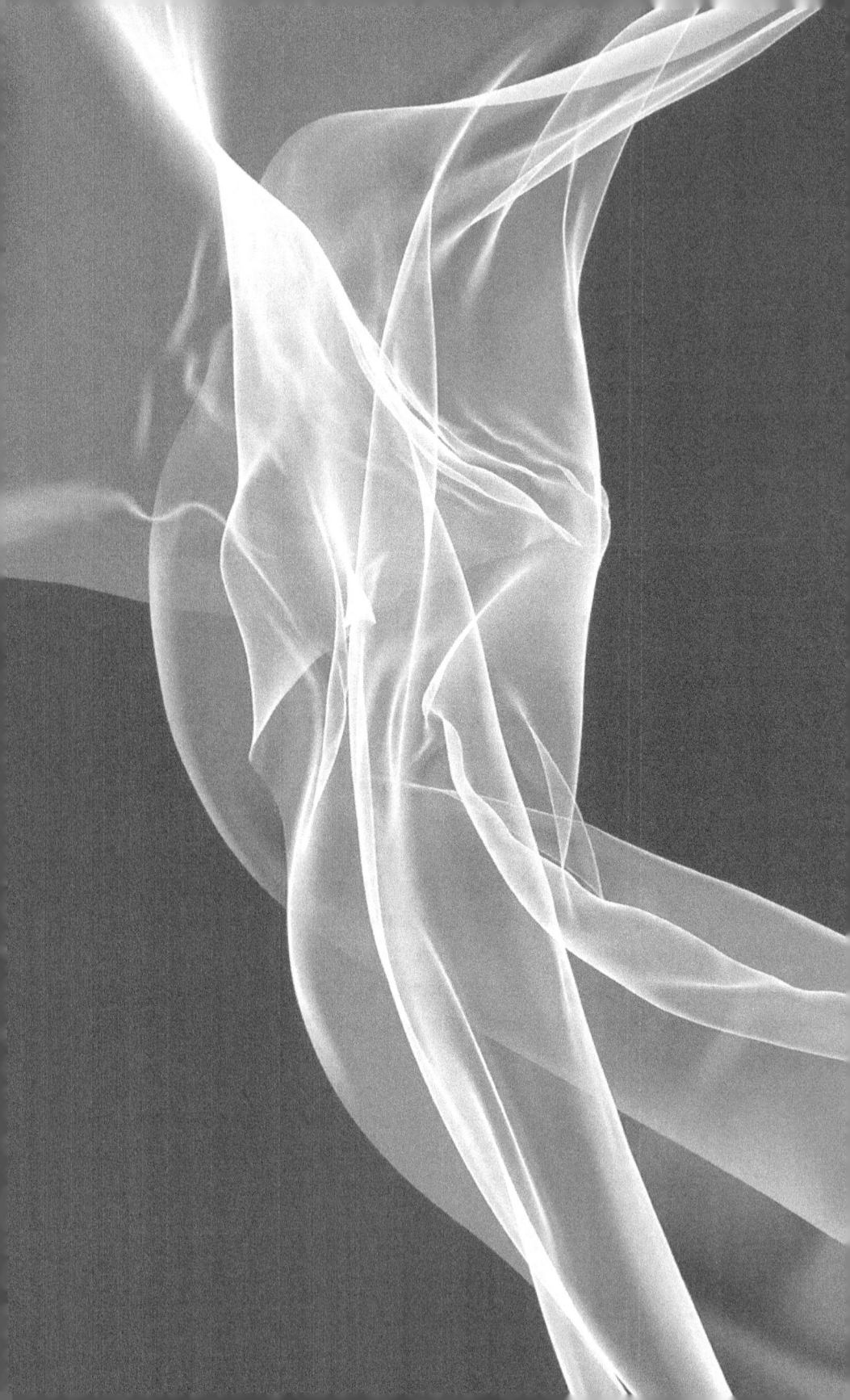

FOREWORD
by Pastor Rachele Dixie

In these pages, you will encounter some of the most transparent and heartfelt stories of women and their journeys through trauma. *Unveiled* pulls back the layers that often shield our eyes and hearts from the depth of what God has brought these women through. It is a testament to the incredible ways God transforms us amidst our tragedies, struggles, and life's most difficult circumstances—experiences many of us never imagined would be part of our stories.

God knows every step of our journey, guiding us with an unyielding hand. All He requires is our trust, for He can use our stories to bring healing and restoration to others. *Unveiled* is a marvelous work—God's work—an opportunity to remember that, whatever you are going through, you are not alone. The stories of these women may be your own or resonate with the experiences of a mother, daughter, sister, friend, or neighbor. Whatever you take from this book, remember this: God unveils us so that He can use us even more powerfully for His glory.

Transparency heals, while judgment cuts and offends. These women choose transparency because they have stood on the other side of judgment. Healed by a God who loves unconditionally, they now extend that same love. God bless Shenita V. Bolton for her vision and obedience to this calling. I believe that this book will inspire you to go deeper with our Lord. Allow Him to do the unveiling, so that He can bring true healing.

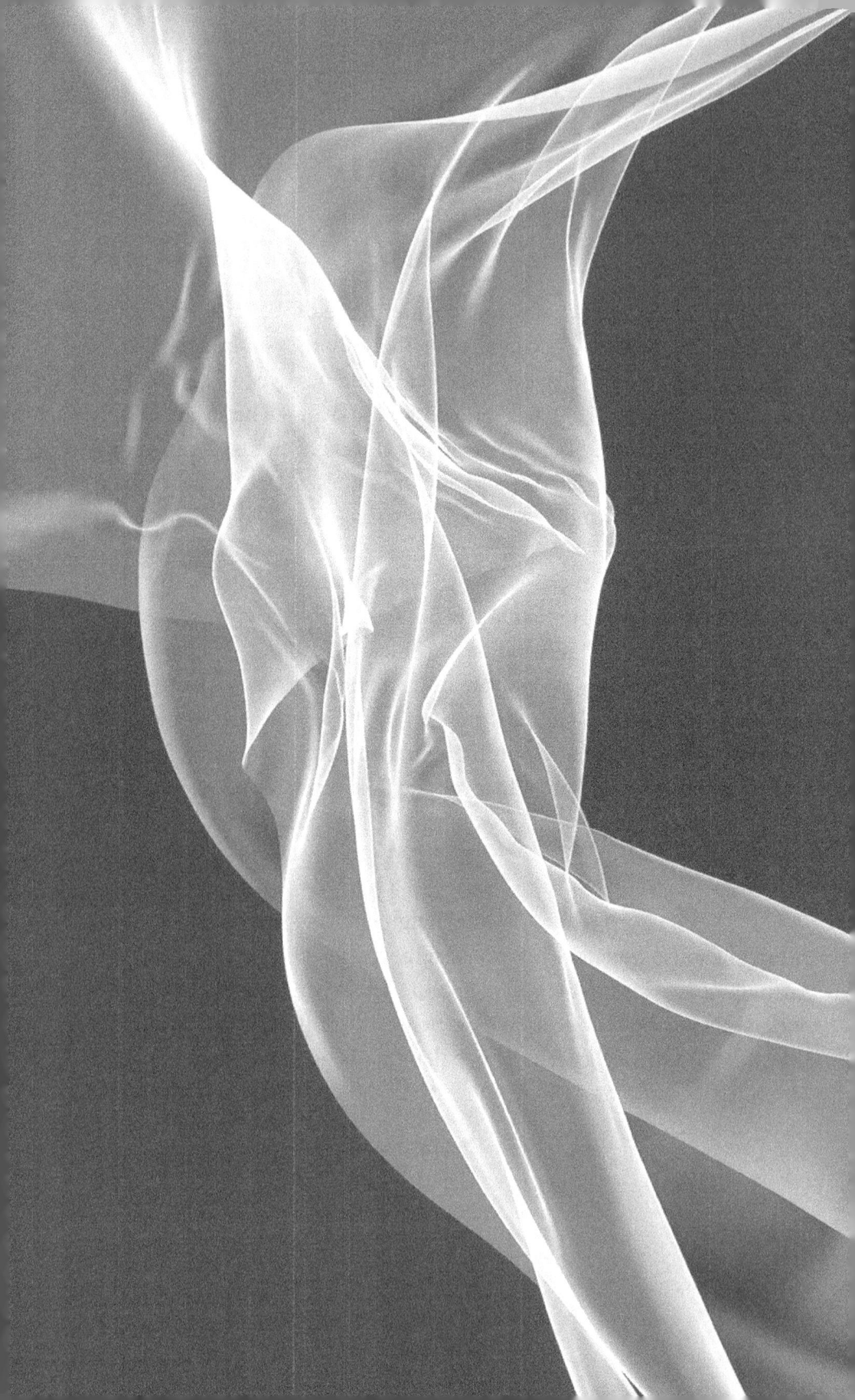

INTRODUCTION

In the quiet stillness of vulnerability lies the profound power of healing. Within the pages of this book, you are invited to journey alongside several courageous women who have bared their souls, sharing stories of trauma and triumph. Each woman, in her own unique way, has navigated or is still facing the depths of her pain, bravely confronting the complex emotions that arise as she unravels the layers of her past.

With hearts as heavy as their burdens, these women found solace in the simple yet transformative act of writing—putting pen to paper to give voice to their silent struggles. Through tears and trembling hands, they paved a path toward healing, guided by an unwavering commitment to help others find solace in the words born from shared experiences.

Their stories are not simply tales of suffering; they are testimonies to the resilience of the human spirit, revealing the unyielding strength within each of us, waiting to be unearthed. As you immerse yourself in these narratives, you will witness the transformative power of vulnerability, the release that comes from illuminating the shadows of the past, and the deep connection that forms when women unite to support and uplift one another.

May these stories serve as beacons of hope for those still navigating the turbulent waters of trauma, illuminating a path toward healing, forgiveness, and, ultimately, self-love. In sharing our stories, we find not only solace for ourselves but also a lifeline for others who may be struggling in their own sea of pain.

Welcome to *Unveiled: Overcoming Trauma to Walk Into Your Divine Purpose*, where the voices of women unite in a chorus of resilience, courage, and healing. Here, these stories are shared in the raw truth of the writers' own words.

1 Thessalonians 5:11

"Wherefore comfort yourselves together, and edify one another, even as also ye do."
King James Version (KJV)

TURN THE PAGE

"Don't be held hostage by your past trauma, it's time for you to …"

TURN

THE

PAGE

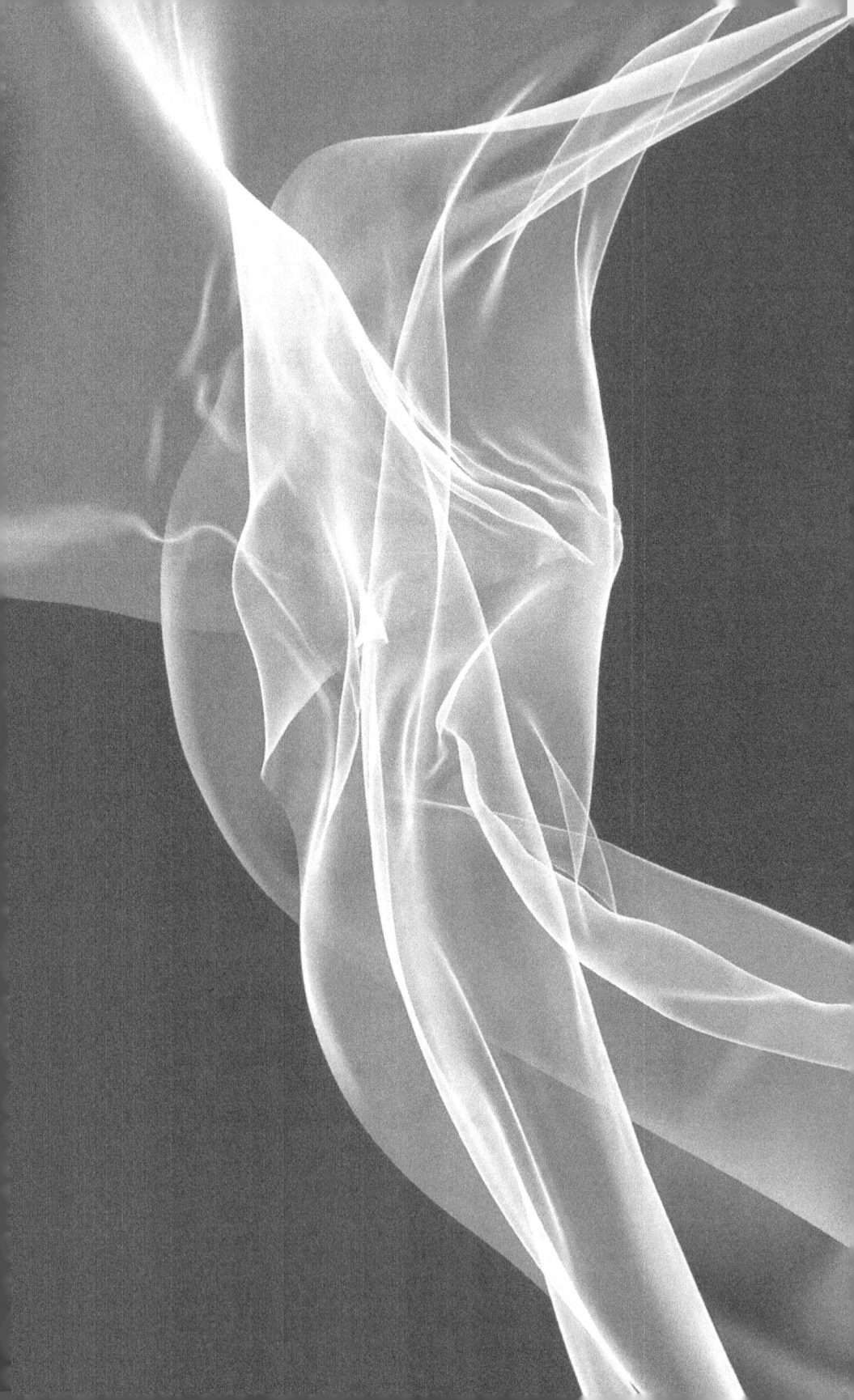

Chapter 1

BEHIND THE FACADE

We live in a society where social media is flooded with carefully curated images of seemingly perfect lives and flawless personas. It's easy to fall into the trap of believing that everyone around us has it all together. But the truth is often quite different. Many women project an image of strength and success while silently carrying deep-rooted trauma, heartache, and pain.

The pressure to appear strong and composed can be overwhelming for women. We're expected to juggle multiple roles and responsibilities—at work, at home, in church, and within our communities. Society's expectation for us to be nurturing, resilient, and emotionally grounded can make it difficult to acknowledge our own struggles and vulnerabilities openly.

Behind the facade of confidence and achievement, many of us silently grapple with past traumas—whether childhood wounds, abusive relationships, personal losses, adult struggles, or self-inflicted pain. These emotional scars often linger, impacting our mental health, relationships, and overall well-being. For some, the fear of judgment or stigma prevents us from seeking help or sharing our inner turmoil. We worry that exposing our pain will make us appear weak, leading us to bury our struggles even deeper and putting on a façade of strength behind what I call the "mask of 'I've got it all together.'"

This constant pressure to maintain a perfect exterior can also create a profound sense of isolation and loneliness. Women who feel compelled to uphold an unblemished image may struggle to form

1

authentic connections, fearing that revealing their true selves will shatter the illusion of having it all together. Yet, vulnerability is not a sign of weakness—it is a courageous act of self-acceptance and healing. Reaching out for support from trusted friends, family, mental health professionals, or spiritual leaders can be a powerful first step toward overcoming trauma and finding inner peace.

As a society, we must work toward creating a more compassionate and understanding environment, one where women feel safe to share their struggles without fear of judgment or shame. By breaking down the stigma surrounding mental health and trauma, we can empower women to embrace their authentic selves and seek the help they need to heal. Ultimately, we must remember that no one has it all together all the time, and it's okay not to be okay.

Behind every facade of strength and success lies a complex, multifaceted individual with her own share of struggles and vulnerabilities. Let us strive to foster empathy, understanding, and support for women who bravely navigate their healing journeys behind the scenes. Together, we can build a more inclusive and compassionate society, where women feel empowered to embrace their imperfections, heal their wounds, and thrive authentically.

Psalms 139:14

"I will praise thee; for I am fearfully *and* wonderfully made: marvelous *are* thy works; and *that* my soul knoweth right well."
King James Version (KJV)

Chapter 2

RAW TRUTH

Speaking the raw truth about trauma is not easy. It takes immense courage to revisit painful memories, relive moments of fear and vulnerability, and expose one's deepest wounds to the world. Yet, powerful women from all walks of life have stepped into the light to share their truths. These women are breaking down the walls of shame and stigma surrounding trauma by telling their stories with unflinching honesty and vulnerability. In doing so, they are reclaiming their voices and power, igniting crucial conversations about healing, resilience, and the transformative strength of speaking one's truth.

Though I am not a therapist or psychologist, I know firsthand that trauma comes in many forms. For too long, women have carried these burdens in silence, bearing the weight of their experiences alone. But more and more, women are finding the strength to break that silence and confront the traumas that have shaped their lives.

One of the most powerful aspects of speaking about our trauma is the sense of faith, solidarity, and empowerment it generates. When one woman bravely shares her story, she creates a ripple effect, resonating with others who have faced similar pain and suffering. This collective voice not only validates the experiences of survivors but also challenges the societal norms and systems that perpetuate and enable trauma.

In speaking our raw truths, we reclaim our narratives and rewrite the stories that have defined us for so long. We refuse to let trauma define us, choosing instead to embrace our resilience, strength, and capacity for healing. By doing so, we break free from the constraints of shame and self-blame, stepping into our power as agents of change and transformation.

As you continue through this book, bearing witness to the stories of women who have spoken out about their trauma, I ask that you read with empathy, compassion, and respect. Listen to these voices, and help create safe spaces for other survivors to share their truths without fear of judgment. Now is the time to stand in solidarity with their struggles and work toward a culture that values and prioritizes healing and justice.

Ultimately, the women who speak their raw truth about trauma are not just sharing stories—they are igniting a revolution. A revolution of empathy, understanding, and empowerment. A revolution that challenges the status quo, demanding a world where all voices are heard, all truths are honored, and all wounds can begin to heal.

Fasten your seatbelt as we journey through powerful stories, poems, and reflections of trauma, hurt, and resilience. Let us stand with these women, learn from their courage, and join them in creating a future where speaking one's truth is not just an act of bravery, but a path to liberation and transformation.

Psalms 34:18

"The LORD is nigh unto them that are of a broken heart; and saveth such as be of a contrite spirit."
King James Version (KJV)

Chapter #3

WHAT GOES ON IN THIS HOUSE
Anonymous

"What goes on in this house, stays in this house!" An infamous line often heard in African American households. In social circles we laugh about it, but for some of us, laughter is only a mechanism to mask the pain that we truly feel deep down inside.

I was 10-years old when it all started. I'd wake up in the middle of the night to a hand either on my breast or down my underpants. I wanted to scream, but I was too afraid of what might happen to me if I did. Most nights, even if I had screamed, there was no one there to protect me. Mom had to work to take care of us kids. Whatever shift was offered, she took it, because that is what she had to do. She left us with someone that SHE trusted, -- but they were not trustworthy. One day, I finally found the courage to tell her what was happening to me, but sadly, nothing changed. She thought that just by telling them to not do it, that they would just stop. BUT IT DID NOT STOP! I was sexually harassed my entire childhood, pre-teen, and teen years, and I still see this person all the time. No acknowledgement of their role in my childhood trauma, no apologies, NOTHING. We just walk around like nothing ever happened – one big happy family. Remember – "what goes on in this house, stays in this house".

God BLESSED me with a WONDERFUL husband to love me through my brokenness. Needless to say, the trauma I experienced took a toll on my marriage in the beginning. But my Love stood by my side. He showed me how to pray my way through. He showed me how to love unconditionally. GOD used him to SHOW ME what it means to truly TRUST my heavenly Father in all situations, whether good or bad.

Today, I am in a place of PEACE! God had delivered me from the trauma of my past. I no longer have nightmares. I no longer harbor hate. I no longer question if my mother really loved me – I know she does. Even today, I look my offender in the eye on a regular basis, and I share the love of Jesus with them. That is what my Heavenly Father expects me to do, and through it all, -- I have PEACE!

Proverbs 3:5-6

"Trust in the LORD with all thine heart; and lean not unto thine own understanding. In all thy ways acknowledge him, and he shall direct thy paths."
King James Version (KJV)

Chapter #4

DOLLAR, DOLLAR, DOLLAR BILLS
Niasha

My mother has always been our source of nurturing stability—our constant. She is beautifully resilient. Married to my father for over fifty-five years, I know their marriage holds memories of love and faithfulness, but I also know it carries the weight of control and a sense of diminished self-esteem he's imposed on her.

Watching and absorbing the dynamic between them has impacted my sister and me deeply. One of my earliest memories of this goes back to when I was about six years old. My father managed every aspect of the household finances. He worked outside the home while my mother was a homemaker. For a short period, she worked part-time at a public library in a nearby neighborhood, and I remember riding with my father to pick her up in the evenings, sitting in the back seat as we waited for her to come down the red brick stairs from the library's back entrance.

Her library job lasted maybe six months to a year. My father eventually told her he preferred that she not work outside the home, saying that her daughters needed her there. So, she quit. My mother was also a skilled seamstress, creating custom women's garments for a close friend who owned a boutique and held fashion shows across the state. She sold her one-of-a-kind pieces, and while it wasn't much, the money helped cover small household items and little things for my sister and me.

By the time I was about twelve, I remember my father would hand my mother an allowance each Friday—usually $50 to $100 for groceries, household items, and gas. The irony of it was in the details: he gave her the money in all one-dollar bills, neatly stuffed in a white bank envelope with a sticky flap closure. I can still picture her pulling that envelope from her purse, carefully counting those dollar bills each week, mentally calculating what remained after each purchase. This ritual was so routine for my sister and me, yet even at that young age, we understood that it was anything but normal. My mother's name wasn't on any of my father's accounts, nor did she have an account of her own. She had a few department store credit cards, which she used for our back-to-school clothes, church dresses, and Christmas gifts, but ultimately, she was financially dependent on him.

As we grew older, my sister and I began to ask her why she put up with this treatment. Why tolerate the disrespect? Why accept being treated like a child by her own husband? It was hard for us to understand. Some of her close friends also knew of the situation and encouraged her to get a job, open a bank account, or even put some of that money aside each week to build a little security for herself.

It wasn't until my teens that I fully realized the symbolism of those dollar bills—small, limited, minimal. It was almost as if he wanted her to feel small, to see herself as less. And yet, my mother was anything but weak. She spoke her mind, and she didn't hesitate to tell him when he was wrong. But his pride, controlling nature, and "I am always right" attitude meant her words went unheard. This dynamic with the one-dollar bills continued for years.

When my mother finally became eligible for Social Security, she no longer needed to rely on his handouts, but the issue shifted. Now he wanted her to turn over her entire Social Security check to him, arguing that it was his career that allowed her to receive that money. She was close to giving in just to maintain the peace, but her friends and my sister and I insisted that she stand her ground.

This struggle over her Social Security continued for months, maybe even years. Eventually, she decided to keep her check in her own bank account, and she has been doing so ever since.

One-dollar bills. Every time I hold one in my hand, I'm transported back to those memories. As a little girl, I was confused by what I saw between my parents, yet a part of me wondered if it was normal. Didn't all families manage money this way? Weren't all husbands as controlling as my father was with my mother? I felt so much sadness for her, and I knew my sister and I had to be her cheerleaders. We tried to lift her spirits, keep her feeling valued, and help her see her own worth.

As a teenager, I started to notice other families—friends whose parents' relationships seemed to be rooted in teamwork, partnership, and mutual respect. I realized then that I would approach life differently. I vowed to have a career, my own money, my own bank account—a sense of security and independence.

Watching my mother depend on my father taught me that there is a healthy kind of dependence a wife should have on her husband, but it should never be rooted in control. When I reached adulthood and started my career, I promised myself that I would always maintain my independence. I would have a career I loved, my own money, buy my own car, live in my own apartment, and eventually buy my own house. I wanted to emulate my mother's strength and grace, but I vowed that my marriage and finances would be different. I didn't want to feel beholden to anyone or accept a man handing me money, whether it was a single dollar or a thousand.

By God's grace and favor, I live the life I dreamed of. If I'm honest, I live the life I wished for my mother. The independence, confidence, and knowledge I've built are things I wish she could have experienced. Despite everything she has endured, her life is beautifully blessed, her faith shines brightly, and her love is a testament to all who know her. She has shown her children and grandchildren what it means to be a Proverbs 31 woman, one whose worth far exceeds rubies.

God placed me in the world of finance and investments, and I don't believe it was by chance. I have learned the importance of budgeting, saving, investing, and building excellent credit. I see how crucial it is for women to play a meaningful role in their household finances. I've been married nearly seven years to a wonderfully loving and humble man. At the beginning, it was a process to let go of my independent lifestyle and fully share a life with him, but I had long since resolved that my marriage would look nothing like my parents'. I did not want to be a woman who lost herself in her husband, who didn't know the state of her own bank account, or who had never owned anything in her own name. I wanted to be a wife who could fully combine her life with her husband's, yet still have a voice in every financial decision we made.

My mother's voice is strong and opinionated, but it was rarely acknowledged by my father. I promised myself I would not be that wife. Looking back on this time in my childhood, I realize that, yes, I experienced trauma. I remember that white bank envelope and its weekly contents vividly, and I remember my mother making every dollar stretch. I remember the pressure she felt in her marriage, constrained by my father's control. Although I have never been physically or sexually abused, watching my mother's experience impacted me emotionally and mentally. Yet, I am thankful. Her life and strength did not turn my heart away from men or make me fear marriage.

The trauma may not be fully healed, but my scars are fading. Prayer, forgiveness, and open conversations have brought me peace. Writing this story deepens my love and respect for my mother. Her resilience is nothing short of miraculous—a reflection of God's hand in her life. She embodies the strength, dignity, and grace of a true Proverbs 31 woman. Her worth is far beyond what fifty or even a hundred one-dollar bills could ever represent.

Proverbs 31:25

"Strength and honour *are* her clothing; and she shall rejoice
in time to come."
King James Version (KJV)

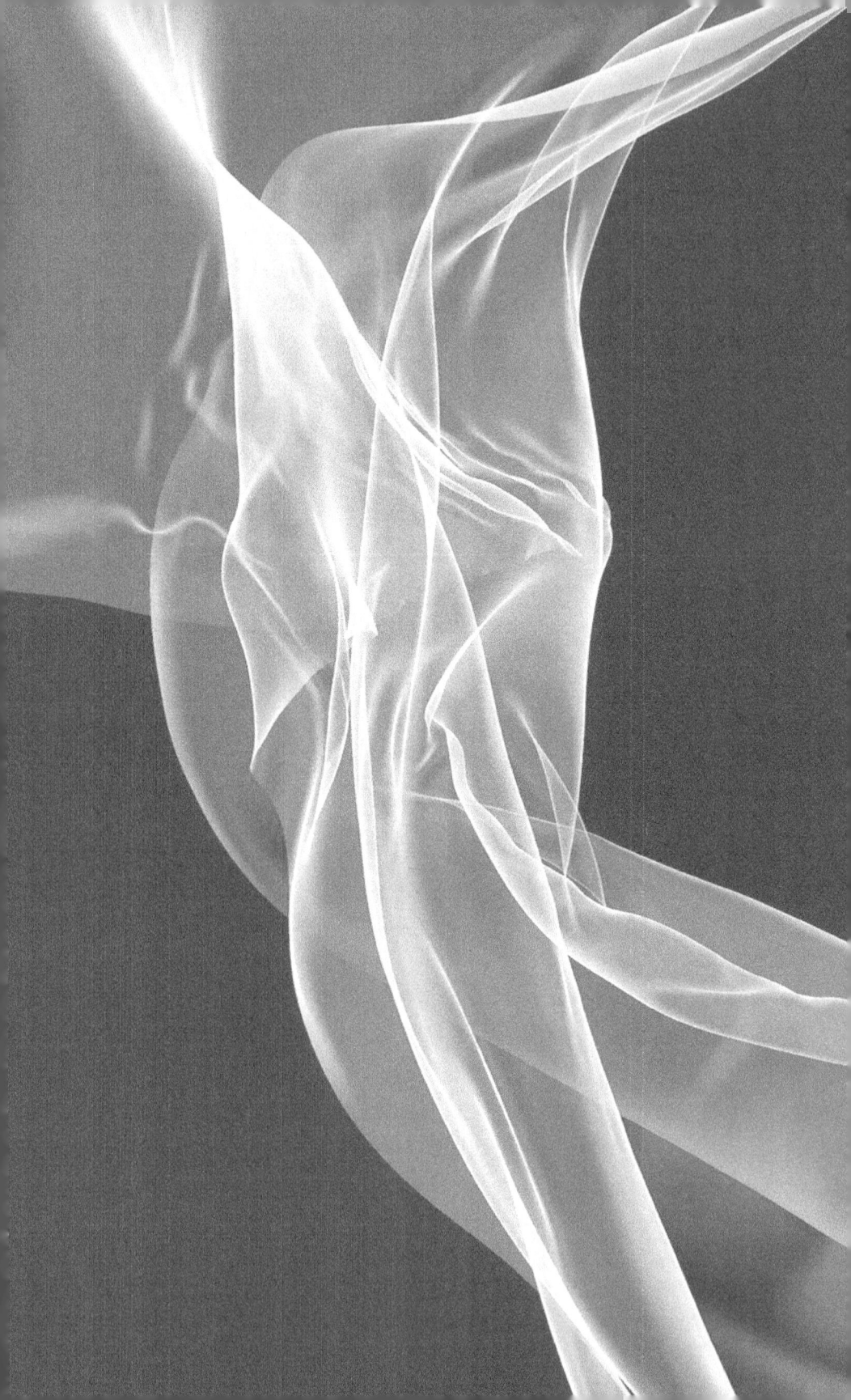

Chapter 5

<u>Who Do I Belong To?</u>
Nita

I grew up in a small town, our home perched on the hilltop of Connersville, Indiana. My mother became pregnant with me at seventeen, and I was born just one month before her eighteenth birthday. She lived with her foster parents, Peggy and Harold, through her pregnancy and for two years after I was born. Peggy and Harold became my loving foster grandparents and raised me as their own.

From a young age, I felt different from other children at school, in our neighborhood, and at church. I didn't live with my mother or father, nor did I carry their last name. In fact, I had no one's last name. My last name was Walker, my mother's maiden name. My mother had taken the name Howard from her husband, my father's name was Parker, and my grandparents' last name was Floyd.

Peggy and Harold showered me with love and care, making sure all my needs were met so that I would never feel alone or abandoned. They explained that my parents were young and unable to care for me, and while I understood, I couldn't help but wonder why I didn't share anyone's last name. I still felt the sting of being different, made worse by the teasing from neighborhood kids: "At least my parents wanted me." Those words cut to the core. And as I grew older, the pain deepened. Both my parents had married and had other children, children they raised and cherished. I couldn't help but ask myself why they wanted my siblings but not me. I knew they loved me in their own way, but I felt hurt, angry, and like an outsider looking in on their lives.

Though I had sadness in my heart for not having my parents by my side, I felt equally blessed to be in such a loving and faithful home where Peggy and Harold poured love and positivity into me. Balancing that sadness with the joy of having them was complicated. As a teenager, I sank into depression, feeling like a puzzle piece that didn't quite fit anywhere. Peer pressures piled on: not having the "right" hair, not fitting in with the "pretty girls," not having the name-brand clothes the "preppy crowd" wore. Adding to my pain was the trauma of being molested by a close family friend. One dark night, feeling overwhelmed by it all, I swallowed a handful of pills, praying to God, "Please don't let me wake up." I just wanted the pain to end. But God whispered, "Not yet, my child." I woke up the next morning with a pounding headache and dizziness, but I was alive. In that moment, I knew God had a greater purpose for me, even if I didn't yet know how I would make it through.

With the love of my foster grandparents, I began to embrace my unique family story, learning to cherish the name that bound me to my heritage. I faced many struggles throughout my life, but with God, my foster grandparents, and the guidance of mentors, I grew into a confident, compassionate woman. That's not to say I didn't still face bouts of depression and insecurity; I did. But God reminded me continually that in Him, I am beautifully and wonderfully made.

Now, over fifty-six years later, I carry the lessons of my past, knowing they've shaped who I am today. My family history is a source of strength and inspiration. Prayer, singing, journaling, and poetry have allowed me to release my emotions and walk confidently in the purpose God has set before me. Here I stand today, healed, ready to write the next chapters of my life and to pour life into others.

Below is a poem I wrote years ago to express the struggle of finding where I truly belonged:

Who Do I Belong To?

In a world of whispers, taunts and pain,
I stand alone, lost in the rain,
A nameless soul in a sea of faces,
A puzzle of identities, tangled laces.

Parker, a father's name, a distant call,
Howard, a stepfather's name, a shadow tall,
Floyd, the foster grandparent's loving embrace,
Yet in their names, I find no solace, I am a puzzle piece out of place.

Children's laughter, like arrows sharp,
Piercing through my fragile heart,
Teasing, mocking, I stand apart,
Lost in a maze, torn apart.

Who am I in this tangled web?
A lost soul, a nameless thread,
Caught between past and present,
A puzzle unsolved, a heart hesitant.

Parker, Howard, Floyd and me,
A tapestry of names, a mystery,
In their echoes, I seek my place
Yearning for belonging, a familiar face.
Confused, hurt, depressed, this can't be real,
Something inside reminds me, I am resilient still,
I search for answers, a void to fill,
In the whispers of the wind, a gentle song,
Guiding me to live a life of FAITH, that's where I belong.

Philippians 4:7

"And the peace of God, which passeth all understanding, shall keep your hearts and minds through Christ Jesus."
King James Version (KJV)

Chapter 6

<u>I REMEMBER - I DON'T REMEMBER</u>
Ashley

I remember the red brick house.
I remember the darkness.
I remember the fear she had.
I remember her cries.
I remember the bruises.
I remember having to hide from you.
I remember her singing, "you are my sunshine."
I remember living in a women's shelter.
I remember when we went back.
I remember the cops.
I remember us leaving again.
I remember being kidnapped.
I remember how strong she had to be.
I remember family begging her to leave.
I remember the apartment we moved into.
I remember the threats you made to her.
I remember moving in with grandma.
I remember not wanting to see you or your mom.
I remember when you finally left her alone.
I remember you going to prison.
I will always remember the abuse.
I will always remember what you did.
I will always remember.

I don't remember birthdays or holidays.
I don't remember you actually being a "father".
I don't remember the inside of that house.
I don't remember my room.
I don't remember being a kid.
I don't remember the laughs.
I don't remember the calmness.
I don't remember any love from you.
I don't ever want to remember.
I don't ever want to remember YOU.

I remember our new start.
I remember the father who stepped in.
I remember her working two jobs.
I remember all the home cooked meals.
I remember her healing.
I remember not having to worry.
I remember the laughter.
I remember the birthdays and holidays.
I remember our family trips.
I remember her coming to all of our events.
I remember her being at every soccer game.
I remember all that she did for us.
I remember all the love she gave us.
I remember her smile.
I remember her.
I remember feeling safe.
Until 2023.

I remember her telling me.
I remember her filing a protection order.
I remember the rush that overcame my body.
I remember having to look at you in court.

I remember the pit in my stomach.
I remember the judge looking the other way, again.
I'll always remember.

I had to grow up quickly, doing my best to help my mom and protect my siblings in every way I could. I pushed the things I witnessed deep down, locking them away in a vault that I've only shared with a few trusted people. My experiences became a way to help others—family, friends, anyone needing support. I've encouraged people to leave abusive relationships, seek professional help, offered a shoulder to cry on, and helped them see the value of their own lives.

I'll never forget my childhood, but I know I'm no longer bound by it. I will always remember being raised by a woman who made her children her life's priority. I will always remember HER.

Philippians 3:13

"Brethren, I count not myself to have apprehended: but *this* one thing *I do*, forgetting those things which are behind, and reaching forth unto those things which are before,"
King James Version (KJV)

Chapter #7

SURVIVING A RARE DISEASE
Jeanetta

My life has been nothing short of extraordinary, marked by both life-altering struggles and unwavering faith. It began with serious complications after my birth, as I struggled with bowel movements. Despite doctors' reassurances, my mother's intuition told her something was wrong. She fought tirelessly until, at age three, I was diagnosed with Hirschsprung Disease—a life-threatening birth defect that prevents the development of nerves responsible for bowel function.

My pediatrician, Dr. Lucian Lewis, referred us to Dr. William L. Donnellan at Children's Memorial Hospital (now Lurie's Children's Hospital) in Chicago. His compassionate care and expertise in abdominal surgery and knowledge of Hirschsprung disease became pivotal in my journey. After multiple surgeries—including a colostomy, ileostomy, and appendix removal—God carried me through, and I was able to live a relatively normal life. At four years old, I was told that my intestines had been stretched as much as possible, and no further surgery could be done. I often joked that God gave my doctor extra skills because, while most people with my condition struggled to gain weight, I've faced the opposite challenge.

My battle with weight has been long and difficult, haunting me so deeply, I opted to undergo gastric sleeve surgery in 2015, which helped me shed about 80 pounds. But as the years passed, the weight returned. In 2022 at my doctor's appointment, as I explained before, it feels like my doctor healed me too well when I was a child. My weight loss doctor suggested trying Ozempic. Despite my insurance not covering it due to my A1C levels being within the normal range of a 5.5 and it had to be over 7 for the insurance to pay, I was determined to give it a try. I was desperate enough to pay the $1,275 out-of-pocket cost, only to switch to Mounjaro in January 2023, which offered a more affordable option by lowering my prescription to $500. With renewed hope, I began to see results as my appetite decreased and the scale moved in the right direction. I was filled with joy and hope once again! However, frequent diarrhea—a common side effect—became a concern, yet I remained optimistic.

As I entered my 50s, it felt like a fresh start. I was focused on my health, empowered, and ready for the next chapter. On July 10, 2023, I had just returned from a cruise with my dear friend, Shenita Bolton, filled with laughter and joy. But that evening, life took a drastic turn. While relaxing with a homemade hamburger, sharp stomach pains suddenly gripped me. I rushed to the bathroom, overtaken by relentless vomiting and diarrhea, which left me feeling utterly drained and frightened.

My symptoms worsened rapidly, and I knew I needed help. I called my mother, but as my condition deteriorated, I dialed 911. By the time the firefighters and paramedics arrived, I was on my knees, unable to stand from the pain. I managed to crawl to the driveway, where they loaded me into the ambulance and rushed me to the hospital.

In the ER, tests revealed I had severe acute pancreatitis, with my lipase enzyme count over 30,000 (normal is 12-52). As the days passed, my condition continued to decline, and my pain was excruciating. During an urgent CAT scan, a new doctor, Dr. William Beck, informed me that I needed emergency surgery. The scan showed a black mass— my intestines, twisted and lifeless. I was told to contact my family because I might not survive. My mind flashed back to childhood memories of Dr. Donnellan's warning about my fragile intestines. The weight of Dr. Beck's words was staggering.

In despair, I called my mother, my unwavering support. Living two hours away, she arrived with a speed fueled by love. Early that Saturday morning, I was wheeled into the operating room, where the surgeon made a precise incision on my abdomen. As my abdominal cavity was opened, my intestines spilled out, blackened and knotted, deprived of oxygen. With remarkable skill, the surgeon began untangling them, carefully irrigating each section. Slowly, life returned to the tissues, transforming from lifeless black to vibrant pink—a miracle unfolding before their eyes.

During surgery, my family and friends gathered in prayer. When I woke up, still on life support and unable to speak, I used notes to communicate with the nurses. Intubated and in constant pain, I lay with my abdomen open, my insides visible beneath a clear plastic wrap due to inflammation.

After three surgeries and five additional procedures, I was given a third chance at life. My pancreas remains dysfunctional, requiring enzymes and insulin for survival, but I am grateful beyond words. When doctors saw no hope, God said, "N0." I've become a walking testament to His power. This journey has shown me that, even in the darkest times, God has the final word. I hold onto my faith and the words of Scripture: "I can do all things through Christ who strengthens me." This is my life, my journey, my Testimony.

Psalms 28:7

"The LORD is my strength and my shield; my heart trusted in him, and I am helped: therefore my heart greatly rejoiceth; and with my song will I praise him."
King James Version (KJV)

Chapter #8

STILL HEALING
Jacque

Childhood trauma? Hmmm, I'm not sure if that's how I see it or not. My first happy memory as a child dates back to when I was three years old. There was a small door in our apartment that led to the attic. I remember that door vividly. My siblings and I were often locked in there, with the couch pushed up against the door, while my mom was gone.

We were given bread to eat, a bucket to pee in and I had my baby doll to hug and hold. I remember being happy about it. At least if I was there, the emotional, physical, and sexual abuse from my father didn't happen. As I got older and realized what happened, it made me sick to my stomach that I was treated that way and was happy to be locked in the attic because it was a place of escape. I would look through the attic window until the daylight was gone, sit in my sister's lap and play with my doll. This became a normal thing for me. I learned very quickly in life that you focus on the positive things and keep it moving.

At 14, I found myself raising a newborn. My sister had taken off with her man, leaving my newborn niece with me. I didn't complain. Mom worked, so I stepped in. I took the baby to high school with me, enrolling her in the daycare program there. For several months, I cared for her as if she were my own, until my sister came back and wanted her child returned.

By the time I was 16, I had graduated high school and found out I was pregnant by a man 30 years older than me. I had always been considered a tomboy, but he was drawn to me and saw the inner beauty I didn't know I had. While I had deep feelings for him, I also realize now that I saw him as a father figure—a father I never really had.

Three months into the pregnancy, I found myself incarcerated. I was charged as an adult for criminal recklessness and possession of a firearm but held as a juvenile. For four months, I sat in solitary confinement in a concrete room with a metal slab for a bed and a toilet. No windows. No people. Nothing. Time blurred. Days and hours merged into a monotonous cycle of isolation. All I knew was that I was behind bars, pregnant, and terrified. During pregnancy, you're supposed to gain weight, but in those four months, I lost 32 pounds. I never spoke to an attorney and had no idea what the future held. I couldn't process what had landed me there, let alone what was to come. Nightmares of what happened haunted me, and when court finally came, my own testimony was used against me as the state's evidence. They didn't understand. I didn't understand. I was sentenced to four years—two suspended—leaving me to serve two but do one. It meant I would give birth while locked up. In my mind, I told myself, "I'm alive. Keep it moving." That was all I could focus on… birth.

The day came while I was at the Indiana Women's Prison. I was sure I was in labor. I called my mom, asking her to come to Indy. I was so grateful she had agreed to take custody of my baby until I could be released. "You probably won't have her today," she reassured me. The guards on my unit echoed her, insisting I wasn't in pain, so I must be fine. From 6 a.m. until the 9:30 p.m. count, I endured. I called my mom again, telling her firmly, "I am definitely in labor." She started making her way. The guards still insisted otherwise.

Around 10 p.m., I went to the bathroom and began pushing on my own. Only then did they call an ambulance. My daughter was born just one block away in the ambulance. No pain meds. No epidural. Nothing. Completely natural at 16 because I didn't "look" like I was in pain. At the hospital, I was chained to the bed and allowed to hold my baby for about three hours before they handed her to my mom. She wasn't born in the prison, so they didn't keep her. The next morning, I was back behind bars. Once again, I told myself, "I'm alive. Keep it moving."

Through it all, I've never felt like a victim. I feel blessed to be alive and to have learned from everything I've experienced. My mother always told me, "God gives the biggest battles to His strongest soldiers."

Now, let's talk about *HEALING*. Healing? My self-love and worth were shattered long before I even knew what they were. As a child, I learned quickly: don't talk back, don't cry, don't sulk. I was the strong one—emotionally and physically. I kept the family moving and together.

With playmates, I didn't fit in. I wasn't dark enough to be Black, nor light enough to be white. I wasn't girly enough for the girls, and that only made me stronger. I became a codependent person, needing to be needed. I could do that! I could fix things. I could be a shoulder to lean on. I didn't have to face my own problems because I was too busy fixing others'! I thought that was my purpose—what I was supposed to do.

As a young adult, I found myself in some messed-up situations, thinking I was doing what I should. Becoming a mother at 16 meant I always had someone who needed me, but even that wasn't enough. I craved being needed because it gave me purpose. It gave me meaning. And for most of my life, I never shared my issues or my past.

In my career, I fixed things—cars, tires, whatever needed repair. In what I thought was my best friendship, I fixed everything. I raised her sons and provided for them financially. That was probably the deepest hurt I've ever experienced. When I needed her, she wasn't there at all.

In relationships, I fixed whatever came up. I was a shoulder to lean on, an escape route for women in horrible relationships they were too scared to leave. I became their crutch, helping them establish themselves, only to be discarded when they no longer needed me.

Each bad "relationship"—whether friendship or romantic—taught me something. I've become stronger at building boundaries and drawing the line. I'm not sure if that has helped me or hindered me, but here I am. At this point in my life, I've forgiven the things that were said and done. I've found peace, even with the pain my biological father caused me since his death.

Still, I've put myself in a bubble—one where no one gets close enough to hurt me, and crazier still, no one gets close enough to really know me. *I am still HEALING.*

Isaiah 41:10

"Fear thou not; for I *am* with thee: be not dismayed; for I *am* thy God: I will strengthen thee; yea, I will help thee; yea, I will uphold thee with the right hand of my righteousness."
King James Version (KJV)

Chapter #9

HOW'S YOUR SPIRIT TODAY? BREATHE!

Tamyra

How is your spirit today? Years ago, I was deeply wounded by people I trusted, cared for, and even served. These were Christians—the church! The betrayal cut so deeply that I didn't know how to process it all. Though I was a Christian, knowing what the Bible says about forgiveness, I didn't think those teachings applied to me. After all, I was the victim.

I clung to scripture like *"They that worship Him must worship Him in spirit and in truth,"* but my spirit and life didn't align with God's Word. I didn't check my spirit, even though I believed in, lived for, and worshipped Jesus Christ.

Being a pastor's kid (a "PK") for over 45 years came with its own unique challenges. I was saved at a young age but didn't develop a close relationship with God until my early twenties. When my dad became a pastor, I was thrust into ministry work—junior usher, choir member, attending Bible study and Sunday school. The spotlight was on me. Everyone seemed to be watching, waiting for me to fail.

At 18, I was criticized for wearing eyeshadow—petty, right? But it made me second-guess myself. Though my parents allowed us to be young and experience life, I didn't want to bring shame to them or the church. So, I acted accordingly. Did I fall short? Yes, many times. But God, in His mercy and grace, protected me even when I didn't know I needed it.

I had a good childhood. My parents provided a stable, middle-class home with love and care. My dad worked tirelessly at a steel factory for over 25 years, never late, and rarely missing a day. I attended public schools, excelled as a student-athlete, and eventually earned a college scholarship to play basketball. After transferring back home to finish college, I embarked on a successful career and later became an Executive Director.

Throughout my journey, I knew God but didn't place my full trust in Him. After college, I met the man of my dreams. We got married and became first-time parents. My husband was successful and well-known in our community. We knew the Lord, but our marriage struggled because we were two head-strong, successful professionals who didn't realize that God should have been at the center of our marriage and everything we did and said in our home and to one another.

That gap allowed the enemy to enter our home. Our lives looked perfect on the outside, but internally, it was a mess—disrespect, discomfort, and disengagement. We prayed separately but rarely together. The enemy had a field day in our marriage.

In life, I was hurt—hurt to the core—by people I trusted. I confided in them, shared my deepest secrets, and they betrayed me. I carried that pain for years, along with the inability to forgive.

Yes, me. A Christian woman. A praise and worship leader. A women's ministry leader. A wife and mother. I held onto anger and bitterness for so long that it consumed me. I became someone nobody wanted to be around—negative, brash, and harsh—because I believed I had the right no to forgive.

But the Word says: *"Let all bitterness and wrath and anger and clamor and slander be put away from you, along with all malice. Be kind to one another, tenderhearted, forgiving one another, as God in Christ forgave you"* (Ephesians 4:31-32).

My mother, a praying woman with a discerning spirit, confronted me about my poor attitude. She told me I needed to forgive, but I resisted. On the outside, I was put together. On the inside, my heart was filthy. Pride told me I had the right to hold onto my hurt, but God hates pride: *"When pride comes, then comes disgrace, but with humility comes wisdom"* (Proverbs 11:2).

In 2016, I was diagnosed with Triple Negative Breast Cancer. The journey was grueling—surgery, six rounds of chemotherapy, and 45 rounds of radiation. My supportive family and friends stood in the gap when I couldn't pray, eat, or even believe for myself.

One day after my sixth chemo treatment, I prayed for healing. I listed every reason I wanted to live, but not once did I ask God to help me forgive. Unforgiveness had become part of my identity. Then I heard Him speak: *"Tamyra, I'll heal you, I'll raise you up to live free so you can, in turn, share your story to help others live free."*

At that moment, I surrendered to God. I prayed and called out the names of those I hadn't forgiven. I let it go—for me. Carrying that burden for 17 years had only hurt me. But when I surrendered, I was free. *"So if the Son sets you free, you will be free indeed"* (John 8:36).

As Christians, we've been programmed to hide our hurts and pains, but we must deal with our traumas and use them to help others. Don't wait for God to force you to listen. I took His grace and mercy for granted, but He gave me the breath to check my spirit.

To anyone holding onto bitterness, anger, or pain—I encourage you to let it go. Release it and live! God desires for us to prosper and be in good health, even as our souls prosper (John 3:2). Nothing—no person, no situation, not even your own struggles—should distance you from God. A strong, close relationship with Him is all that truly matters. God has a divine plan for your life, but to fulfill it, we must be willing to endure until the end. Each day, we are called to discipline ourselves in His Word and train our spirits to align with His will, not only for our own benefit but also to show love and kindness toward one another. So today, make the choice: Let it go and live!

Finally, I encourage you to check yourself—spiritually, emotionally, and physically. I believe the stress I carried contributed to my cancer. Today, I am several years cancer-free, and my spirit is free because I let go of the unnecessary weight in my heart.

God is the Redeemer.

Signed,
A Sister Who Wants You Free!

John 8:36

"If the Son therefore shall make you free, ye shall be free indeed."
King James Version (KJV)

Chapter #10

<u>THE COLLISION</u>
Nita

It was a beautiful summer morning when I climbed into the family car, excitement bubbling inside me. We were setting out from Indiana to California for our family reunion—my grandparents, Aunt Mary, my little cousin Terry, and me. The road stretched ahead, framed by green trees, mountains, and endless possibilities. I loved road trips; they were filled with music, laughter, Grandma's fried chicken, Aunt Mary's pound cake, snacks, and the thrill of adventure.

This would be our longest trip yet, and I was ready for every stop to explore caves, parks, and other sites. As we cruised along the highway, I glanced over at Terry, who was playing with his toys, while my grandparents and aunt chatted about life, family, and politics. I felt safe, surrounded by love and warmth.

Then, suddenly, the calm shattered. My grandmother murmured, "We've come to the end of the barrels," as we exited a construction zone in Wyoming. And then it happened—a semi-truck came barreling toward us, slamming into our car with a jarring force. In an instant, we were propelled forward, the world outside blurring as we were pushed fifty feet into oncoming traffic. Panic gripped my heart as the car spun wildly, putting us directly in the path of an oncoming truck.

"JESUS, JESUS, JESUS!" I screamed, my voice cutting through the chaos and fear. I clutched Terry tightly, eyes wide and heart pounding, praying for safety. The car tilted, balancing precariously on two wheels before finally crashing back down.

When the car stopped, silence fell. The pungent smell of gasoline filled the air, a stark reminder of how close we had come to death. Tears streamed down my face as I looked around, my heart racing. I saw blood covering my grandmother, and my stomach dropped, fearing she was gone. I shook her gently, pleading with her to wake up.

My grandfather groaned in pain, clutching his side. My grandmother lay slumped over, blood trickling down her face. My aunt was motionless, her neck at an unnatural angle, and little Terry whimpered, his ankle twisted oddly.

Fear and gratitude washed over me all at once. At eleven years old, I somehow knew that God had wrapped His arms around me, sparing me from harm. I knew that calling on the name of Jesus had made a difference for my family.

"Help is coming!" I called out, even as I cried. Unbuckling my seatbelt, I crawled over to Terry, cradling his head. "It's okay, Terry. You're going to be alright." Soon, the sound of sirens filled the air, and voices from outside the car gave instructions as people rushed to help. I saw my grandmother begin to stir and step out of the car. I took a deep breath, a wave of calm washing over me as I whispered, "Thank you, Jesus, for keeping us safe."

The paramedics arrived and worked quickly, assessing injuries and offering comfort. I watched them tend to each family member, feeling my heart swell with hope. I knew I had to be strong for them, even as I was just beginning to understand the magnitude of what we'd gone through.

As they loaded us into ambulances, I held Terry close, singing to him and reassuring him, "You're brave, Terry. We'll get through this together." Despite the pain and fear, hope warmed my heart, knowing that our faith would see us through.

In the weeks that followed, my Aunt Mary remained in the hospital, and the rest of us recovered at a nearby hotel. My grandmother and I found solace in prayer. She shared our story with family and friends over the phone, her voice steady as she said, "It was God who saved us. I know it."

As an eleven-year-old girl, I looked around at my family—bruised, broken, battered, but alive—and realized our journey wasn't over. We remained in Wyoming for several weeks and eventually made it to California, but this was a journey not only of miles but of faith and resilience. I learned a powerful lesson that day: the strength of calling on Jesus in moments of fear, and the love that binds a family together.

I carry this experience with me, a constant reminder of how precious life is and how faith can truly move mountains.

Romans 10:13

"For whosoever shall call upon the name of the Lord shall be saved."
King James Version (KJV)

Chapter #11

<u>HE'S NOT YOUR FATHER</u>
Neco

I first encountered the reality of childhood trauma at thirteen. I was playing outside with my cousins, and when it was my turn to ride the bike, I didn't want to stop. One of my older cousins grew frustrated and snapped, "That's why Uncle Charles isn't your real father!" Her words hit me like a punch. I dropped the bike, ran into the house crying, and told my mom what had happened. She hugged me and said, "Let's wait until your dad comes home, and then we'll talk."

When my dad arrived, my mom gently told him what happened. He sat down beside me, took my hand, and said, "Your mother and I were waiting until you turned sixteen to tell you. We're sorry you found out this way." Then my mom shared the story: she was eighteen and newly pregnant when she met my dad, who wasn't my biological father. My biological father had left her, and the man I'd always called "Dad" stepped in, loving her and choosing to raise me as his own. He promised her he'd take care of me as if I were his own flesh and blood, and he had kept that promise. Yet, despite all of this, the pain remained.

I couldn't shake my cousin's words. Who would be so cruel as to say something like that to a child? The hurt stayed with me, and I knew I needed answers. At twenty-two, I finally met my biological father. It was awkward, but I needed closure. "Why did you leave me?" I asked. His answer surprised me: "The life I was living was no place for a child. The man who loved your mom could give you what I couldn't—love." I was left feeling emotional, lost, and confused. I didn't ask to be here, yet I felt like my mom had been wronged. It took years to work through those emotions. But by God's grace, I came to understand.

Everything happened exactly as it needed to. I had to realize that my trial held a purpose—it prepared me for my future. The father who raised me instilled in me values, morals, and principles. God placed him in my mother's life because He knew what I'd need to face in adulthood.

Through prayer, I asked God to reveal my purpose. The Holy Spirit showed me that if I wanted to move forward, I needed to forgive my biological father for not being there and embrace the man who chose to be my father. Once I forgave, God took care of the rest. God sends us what we need; the enemy sends what we want.

We've all made mistakes, and when you know better, you do better. Just because someone has hurt you doesn't mean they're a bad person. We are all imperfect beings, trying our best.

YEARS LATER... Life brought new challenges, and unfortunately, my marriage hit a breaking point. We opted to part ways. That experience forced me to refocus and finally prioritize my own well-being. I started small acts of self-care: noticing five beautiful things on my commute, helping others by opening a door or carrying a bag, checking in with my emotions, journaling, choosing who I spent time with, and treating myself to small luxuries.

I also decided to take my first solo trip to Jamaica. I wanted to explore myself on my own terms. I went snorkeling, took a party boat, dined out, and even explored Margaritaville, all by myself—and had the time of my life! I met new people, tried new things, and found healing in the beautiful blue ocean. I felt God's peace washing over me, filling me with self-love and gratitude as I reflected on my new life, with no regrets.

Lessons are meant to grow us so we don't repeat the same mistakes. I am grateful for every lesson, every detour, and every moment of reflection that led me to the woman I am today.

Excerpt from "Divorce: Just a Detour to Your Destination" by Neco Beasley, the Ultimate Divorce Workbook.

James 1:2-3

"My brethren, count it all joy when ye fall into divers temptations;
Knowing this, that the trying of your faith
worketh patience."
King James Version (KJV)

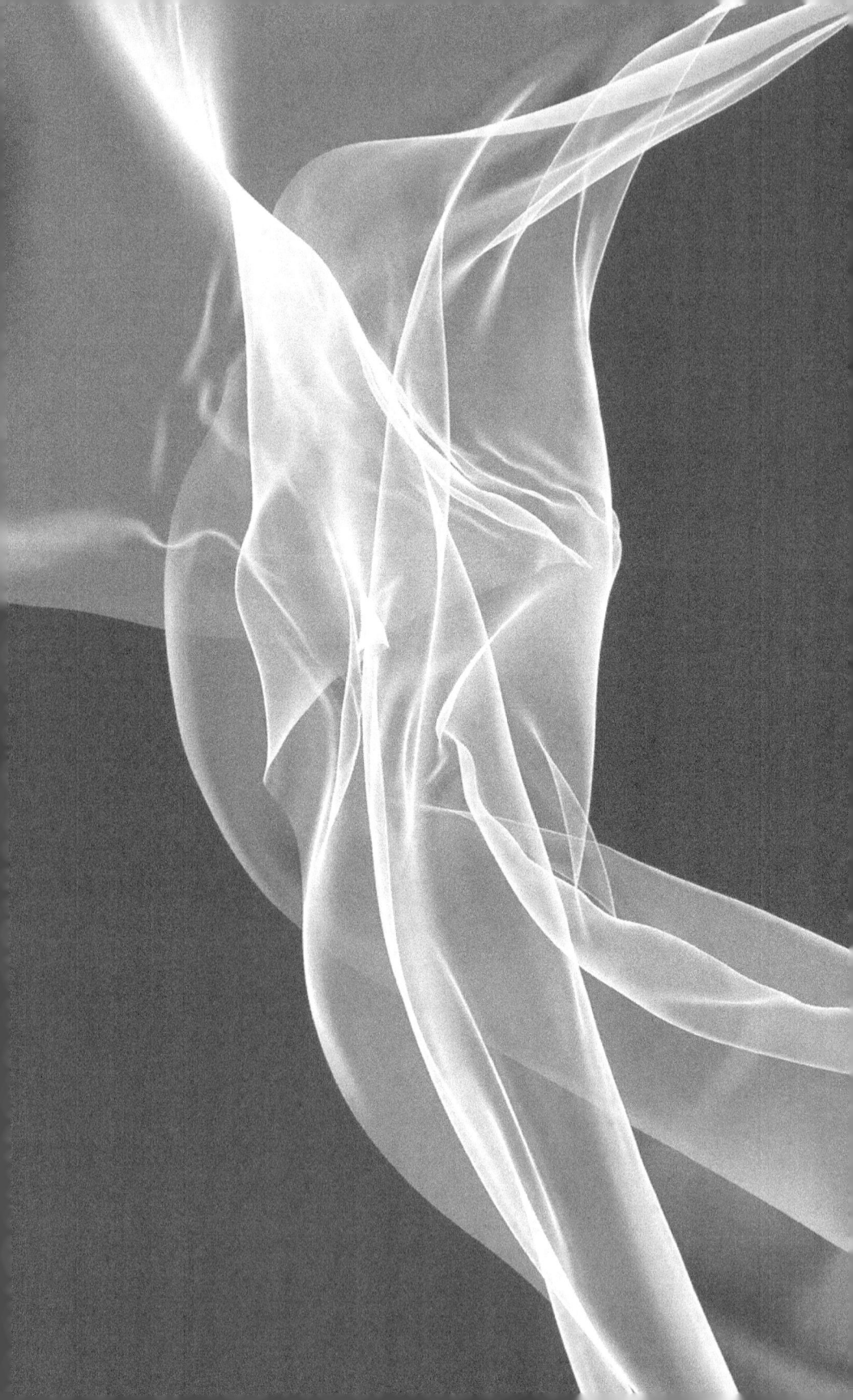

Chapter #12

THE FATHER I'VE ALWAYS WANTED
THE FATHER I'LL ALWAYS HAVE
Kela

As I reflect back over my life, I can honestly say I had a happy childhood. Growing up on Carver Drive in Muncie, Indiana, I remember riding my Huffy bike with my friends, sitting on the porch with neighbors listening to music, laughing, and watching cars pass by. I remember walking to the little park in our neighborhood, always making sure to return home before the streetlights came on. My mother would lay out our church clothes, and we attended services several days each week. Summers were often spent with extended family in Tennessee or Ohio, and I cherished the annual trip to Tuhey Pool and Vacation Bible School at church.

My mother worked hard to provide for us as a single parent. I never went without food or clothing. Yet, for all the happy memories, one thing was missing—my biological father. He was not present for school events or daily life. My mother was careful about who she allowed around us, so there were no random men or boyfriends in our home. When I was nine or ten, my mom introduced me to the man who would become my stepfather. He seemed nice at first, even inviting us over to his apartment and cooking my favorite food—chili with cheese. It wasn't long before they secretly married, and I had a stepfather I didn't care for. Some might think I didn't want to share my mother, but that wasn't it—I simply didn't have a good feeling about him, even though I couldn't quite articulate why.

As time went on, I saw how he hurt my mother, not physically but emotionally and mentally. He was a minister, and it felt like we lived a double life—the kind he presented at church and the one that played out at home. He'd say hurtful things, hide household items (irons, telephone, etc.), and sometimes not want my mother to work or go out. Occasionally, he'd have angry outbursts that left me so angry I once grabbed a butcher knife, thinking I could stand up to him. I couldn't, of course, and that anger eventually led me to steal my mother's car and "run away" to my godmother's house. My mother, knowing me well, had already alerted them, and they were waiting for me.

Their relationship had its ups and downs, even ending in a secret divorce and later a remarriage. During that time, I began longing for a connection with my biological father, Keith Johnson. My mother never spoke negatively about him, but Keith (as I called him) made little effort to build a relationship with me. He lived only about fifty miles away in Indianapolis, so distance wasn't the issue. When I did see him, I felt his love, but he never followed up. By the time I was eleven or twelve, I felt the sting of rejection.

Once, Keith came by late at night with a bag of clothes for me. I remember that black garbage bag smelling like cigarettes, and inside was a canary-colored outfit I wore to church often. That outfit was one of the few gifts he ever gave me. With emotional turmoil at home and the longing for a relationship with my father Keith, rejection started to take root in my heart.

At fifteen, while on a trip to Indianapolis with my mom, I grew frustrated, accusing her of keeping me from my father. She insisted that was far from the truth, as she tried over and over to reason why we needed to get home to Muncie. I got beside myself and yelled at her for not letting me see him. Eventually, my mom reluctantly gave in and took me to see him.

That was nearly thirty years ago, yet I still vividly remember standing outside that dark, spooky duplex, waiting for what felt like forever. No one answered the door. Finally, a neighbor came out and asked if we were there for "Big John"—my father's nickname. Without hesitation, he walked us straight into my father's house and told us to wait.

Those fifteen to twenty minutes felt like the longest of my life. The house was dark and scary, with the sound of dogs barking from the basement. When my father and stepmother eventually came downstairs, their conversation was disjointed and made no sense. I'll never forget my stepmother asking my mother how her maternal grandmother was doing. My response was sharp and immediate: I pointed out that my maternal grandmother had died a long time ago—eight years, to be exact. "Now, you know you're high if you're asking about dead people," I thought bitterly.

We left in a hurry, tears streaming down my face. My mother's words as we drove away still echo in my mind: "And that's why I didn't want to take you over there." She had known the lifestyle they lived and had tried to shield me from it, but the truth was laid bare that night. I realized then that my father was a drug addict, and once again, rejection settled heavily on my heart. If he truly loved me, why couldn't he get clean? Why wasn't I enough?

Throughout high school, I tried to fill that void. I was active in church, did well in school, and had big dreams, but the ache for my father lingered. My mother and stepfather divorced during my high school years, and then it was off to college. Despite outward success, the seeds of rejection continued to grow.

After a few years, I lost contact with my father. In April of 2001, I finally spoke to him, but the conversation was far from the heartfelt reunion I had imagined. Outwardly, it was rude, disrespectful, and belligerent; yet, deep inside, it was the little girl in me crying out for her dad. Silence between us wasn't unusual—it was the norm. He was never consistently present in my life, which is why I now cling to the few memories I have of being with him.

In September of 2001, I made another attempt. I don't remember if it was for his birthday or just a random call, but I reached out. It was my way of extending an olive branch, another attempt to claim what I had never truly experienced but desperately yearned for—a real relationship with him. After the call, I calmly told my mom, "He's not interested. I'll never call him again."

Just one week later, he suffered a medical emergency and passed away shortly after. Before his passing, I whispered in his ear that I forgave him. At his funeral, I cried a lot of tears—not because he was gone, but for the years of rejection and hurt, missed connection, and the relationship we would never have.

My journey of dealing with rejection and sadness has felt like living with a dormant virus in my body. It's something you think is gone until it suddenly flares up and makes you sick. The truth is, the virus was always there, just lying dormant. Dormant, by definition, means temporarily inactive or inoperable, but with the potential to become active again. That's exactly what rejection felt like in my life—an underlying issue that would resurface unexpectedly.

I graduated from college, built a successful career, married the love of my life, and stayed active in my community. From the outside looking in, I was living a "prosperous and healthy life." Yet, deep within, the dormant virus of rejection still lingered. Around the second or third year of my marriage, it reactivated. My husband and I had an argument, and he raised his voice. I can't even remember what the argument was about, but I know I screamed at him, "You're not my father!" The next thing I knew, I was on the floor, crying uncontrollably. It was then that I realized I was still angry—angry at a man who was no longer alive. I thought I had moved past it, but I hadn't.

I was mad at my stepfather for the emotional pain he caused, and mad at my father for abandoning me. In my mind, he could have stopped everything I went through. In reality, my father's presence might not have been what I idealized. But that was my perspective, and those were my feelings. Year after year, I wrestled with those emotions, but through consistent prayers for healing, understanding, and forgiveness, I began to find peace.

A few years ago, I ran into my stepfather. I greeted him kindly, and to my surprise, there wasn't a single trace of bitterness in my heart. I didn't think about stabbing him, shooting him, or poisoning him— thoughts that had crossed my mind in my darkest moments. I spoke to him genuinely and kept it moving. That peace didn't come easily. It came from being honest with myself, praying to the Lord, and seeking professional help.

Over time, I came to understand that my father struggled with addiction his entire life. It was a sickness he couldn't overcome. In the last year of his life, he tried to get clean, but the damage from years of drug use and failing health ultimately claimed him at the age of 54. My older brothers and other family members have always told me how much he loved me, but I never felt it for myself. I now realize that addiction robbed him of the ability to show it the way I needed. Perhaps, in his mind, keeping me away was his way of protecting me from the life he lived.

To anyone struggling, I want you to know that it's okay to admit you're "not okay." You don't have to hide behind a mask or pretend everything is fine. For years, I struggled with my identity, acceptance, and feeling wanted. It even impacted my faith, making me doubt that God truly loved me or that I was good enough for His blessings. But I am a living witness that Psalm 27:10 is true: "When my father and my mother forsake me, then the LORD will take me up." And Psalm 147:3 reminds us, "He healeth the broken in heart, and bindeth up their wounds."

I never had the earthly father I longed for, but I have a Heavenly Father who is consistent, loving, strong, and faithful. He fights my battles and never leaves my side. Do I still have challenging days? Yes. Do waves of grief come where I miss my father? Absolutely. Do I second-guess myself sometimes? Yes. Do I feel abandoned at times? Yes. But have I grown and matured? Without a doubt. Am I bitter? No.

When I reflect on some of my adult behaviors, I can see how they were shaped by the rejection I felt. But God is redefining me. Even when those feelings of rejection or longing for acceptance arise, I am learning to resist negative thoughts and rest in the confidence of the Lord.

For all the times I sought comfort in external things and people, I now look to God for my healing, my identity, and my peace. I stand on Deuteronomy 31:8, which says, "Do not be afraid or discouraged, for the LORD will personally go ahead of you. He will

be with you; He will neither fail you nor abandon you." I know I can count on God. He has never abandoned me, and He never will.

I may not have had the father I dreamed of, but I am forever grateful for the **Father I'll always have**.

1 John 3:1

"Behold, what manner of love the Father hath bestowed upon us, that we should be called the sons of God: therefore the world knoweth us not, because it knew him not."

King James Version (KJV)

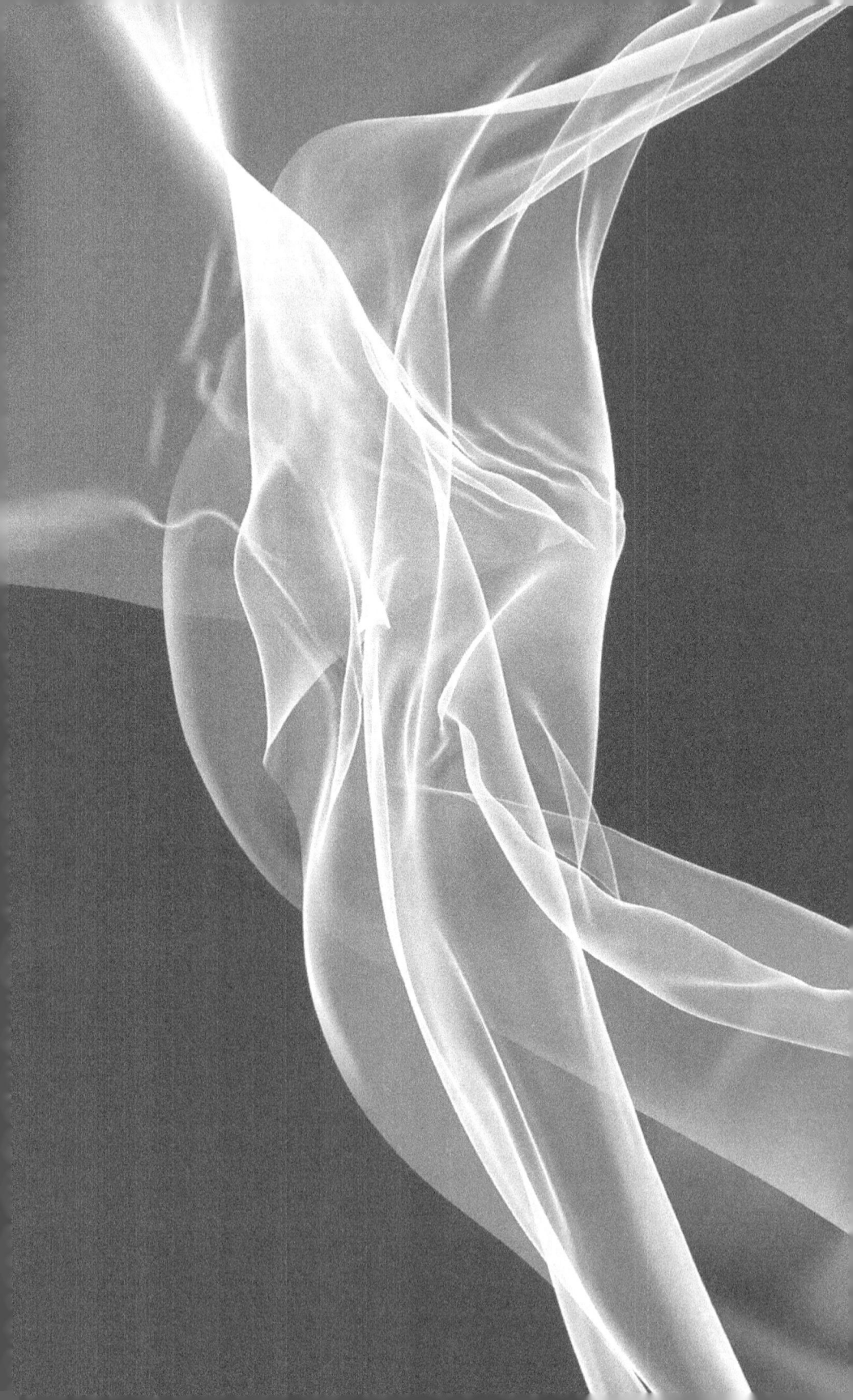

Chapter #13

RESTORED
Anonymous

As a child, I knew God was real, and I loved Him deeply. Even though I couldn't fully understand it then, I wanted to be who He created me to be, and I desired the life He wanted for me.

Around the age of ten, I found myself in a situation I didn't understand spiritually. An older cousin encouraged me to connect with her in ways that, while confusing, felt physically pleasant at the time. I now see that experience wasn't aligned with God's will. That early experience of physical affection misdirected my understanding of love and connection. For a long time, I believed that physical pleasure was the measure of love, rather than intimate conversations, friendship, or true connection. And, if I'm being honest, it was all too often just a sexual experience. I pray that no young girl or boy ever goes through that first intimate physical experience whether it is male to male, female to female, or male to female, believes that physical pleasure is what defines love.

When we visited my aunt and uncle, I felt a hidden expectation that I had to be physical with her. She would wait until my other sisters were asleep, then come close to me and tell me to do things to her that required me touching her and experiencing pleasure. As you can imagine this led me to a secret life of lusting after other women. I have engaged in self-pleasuring as a means to fulfillment. These experiences set me on a path of confusion, one that eventually led me into a hidden life of struggling with desires I couldn't reconcile. In my private battles, I sought fulfillment in ways I knew weren't aligned with my faith.

For most of my life, I kept all of this to myself, trying to live as though I was fully aligned with God's will and living a Godly life. However, I often found myself caught up in sexual thoughts that were certainly not of God. This battle continued through my twenties, thirties, forties, and even into my fifties. My life has been lived in covert homosexuality.

I found myself entangled in a 17-year relationship that stripped away the essence of who God had called me to be. On the surface, it appeared to be nothing more than friendship, but it was so much more. I worked hard to keep it hidden, and for the most part, I succeeded. If anyone suspected the truth, they never said a word. No one challenged me about the inappropriateness of the relationship, perhaps because I wore the mask of secrecy so well.

I had become consumed by the need to please someone who had no regard for my spiritual struggle or desire to live a Godly life. I was trapped in a cycle of trying to mold myself into something I was not, compromising my values and identity for the sake of someone else's approval. If I didn't meet her expectations, I was labeled a hypocrite. Ironically, she wasn't wrong. I was living a double life—serving in the church, loving the Lord, and genuinely wanting to please Him, while simultaneously being bound by a relationship that pulled me further away from His will.

Pleasing a person who cared nothing for my walk with God had absolutely nothing to do with living a Godly life, and yet, I allowed it to dominate my existence.

Over time, I felt a calling to pull away from those desires and find a way back to who I knew God wanted me to be. When the relationship ended, it was a painful and volatile breakup, and I found myself alone and unsure of how to reconnect with the path I was meant to walk. Through tears and brokenness, I began a journey of healing. Over these past few years, God has been restoring me, taking away desires and replacing them with peace and a renewed purpose. He's shown me that there is so much more He wants me to do for His Kingdom.

I share this without judgment of anyone who may be walking a similar path because I genuinely understand the weight of these struggles with a homosexual lifestyle. I remain open to conversations about this journey and pray continually for God's strength. I know that any of us can fall, but I also believe in the power of restoration. If I can ever be of help to someone else, I am here, willing to share what God has done in my life.

My story of healing and restoration is still unfolding, but I walk forward each day with a sense of peace, knowing that God has a plan and a purpose for me.

Romans 12:1-2

"I beseech you therefore, brethren, by the mercies of God, that ye present your bodies a living sacrifice, holy, acceptable unto God, *which is* your reasonable service. And be not conformed to this world; but be ye transformed by the renewing of your mind, that ye may prove what is that good, and acceptable, and perfect will of God."
King James Version (KJV)

Chapter #14

LOSING MY SON
Anonymous

My life has been one of hope and heartache. My son was my pride and joy, with an infectious laugh and an energy that could light up any room. But as he grew older, shadows began to overtake him. Friends who once shared dreams with him drifted onto dangerous paths, and in his search for belonging, he was pulled into the world of drugs.

I watched helplessly as my son changed. The little boy who once ran through the yard, full of dreams and laughter, was now ensnared in addiction. I tried everything—conversations filled with love, tears, and desperate pleas for him to break free. Yet, the more I tried, the deeper he seemed to sink. He became a person I could hardly recognize, yet my love for him never wavered.

Then, one night, I received the call that shattered my world. My son had been caught in the crossfire of senseless violence. That tragic moment took him from me, leaving a void that nothing could ever fill. Even as I write these words, tears fall because the ache of missing him is beyond anything words can capture. The news of his death felt like a physical blow, and I let out a scream I didn't even know was within me. The pain was sharp, cutting through every fiber of my being.

The days that followed were a blur of grief. Family and friends offered their condolences, but I was numb, unable to hear or feel anything. I walked around in a fog, struggling to comprehend the reality of his absence. Every corner of my home held memories of him; even in my other children, I saw traces of him. I turned inward, drowning in my sorrow.

Then one day, I realized I had to trust God through it all. I had always believed in God, always felt that we had a close relationship, but now my faith was truly being tested. Everything I had ever spoken about faith was now put to the test, and I had to find my refuge in God. I began spending intentional time in prayer, pouring out my heart in the quiet of night.

One night, as I knelt in prayer, a warmth washed over me—a quiet peace amidst the sorrow. In that moment, I realized that while my grief was deep, it would become just a little lighter each day. God showed me that I didn't need to rush through my grief; I just needed to trust Him to carry me through it. Slowly, I began to see that while my son's life had its struggles, it was also filled with moments of love and joy.

I am still grieving, but each day I am healing. Though my son is not with me physically, he remains with me in spirit and in my heart.

Matthew 5:4

"Blessed are they that mourn: for they shall be comforted."
King James Version (KJV)

Chapter #15

NAVIGATING UNPREDICTABLE <u>STORMS</u>
Nita

As a little girl, I was full of life, with a world of thoughts swirling in my mind. Raised by loving grandparents, I knew warmth, laughter, and safety. Their home was filled with the aroma of southern cooking, the heat of a pressing comb, and the sound of gospel music—a comforting contrast to the chaotic world outside.

Visits to my father's home or my mother's brought entirely different realities. Like any child, I longed for a deep connection with my father, but I was always met with shadows. What little girl doesn't want to have a special relationship with their father? My father, a man with a ***VERY GOOD HEART*** at his core, was consumed by his own demons, often unpredictable and stormy. Thankfully, I had a kind and loving stepmother who embraced me as her own. It was during one of my visits with my father and stepmother that the storm unleashed its fury.

Every fiber of my being was filled with excitement for the visit because my stepmother had just brought my precious baby sister into the world. I arrived to see her cradling her third child—or her fourth if you counted me. My sweet baby sister's soft coos and tiny cries filled the air, a melody of new life and hope. But the happiness was short-lived. That evening, my father stumbled through the door, reeking of alcohol. My heart sank as the tension in the room escalated as he tried to take the rent money from the dresser drawer to buy more liquor.

My stepmother's soft, pleading voice tried to hold the peace. "Please don't take that money. We need it to pay the rent," she said, her tone calm but weary. My father's slurred, venomous words cut through her like a blade. "Why can't you just be quiet for once and let me do what the hell I want to do?" he roared, his face contorted with rage. She stood firm, her resilience shining through, but her calm only seemed to stoke his anger further. I felt my skin crawl with fear as their argument escalated, the walls closing in around me.

Then it happened. In a flash of fury, my father grabbed an umbrella leaning against the wall and swung it at my stepmother. The heavy fabric struck her chest—the very chest that nourished her baby girl, my sister. I froze, my breath stolen by the shock of what I had just witnessed. Tears streamed down my face as I ran between them, my voice trembling but loud as I screamed, "Get the hell out and leave her alone!" In that moment, a child was forced to become a protector, a defender for someone who had always cared for me.

I had never witnessed violence like this. The image seared itself into my memory, a violent contrast to the peaceful life I cherished with my grandparents. Summoning all my courage, I pushed my father away from my stepmother and screamed again, "Get out now." I stood frozen in fear, afraid I would be hit next, afraid the man I longed to have in my life would hate me, afraid his rage would spiral further. But as he looked into my eyes, I caught a fleeting glimpse of hesitation—perhaps even fear. He turned and walked out the door.

That night, as I lay in bed, sadness and confusion consumed me. While I cherished the love and care I received from my grandparents, I couldn't shake the longing for my biological parents' love. Why was my father like this? The question haunted me.

Visits to my mother's home offered a different kind of complexity. I would watch her from a distance as she stared at her reflection in the mirror. Her expression was a mix of longing and defeat, as though she were searching for something she couldn't find. On some days, she smiled at me, but it was a smile that never fully reached her eyes. I felt a deep ache in my heart, sensing the battles she fought silently within.

As a child, I wanted to ask her why she didn't see her own beauty. To me, my mother was beautiful. But deep down, I knew her past traumas whispered lies to her soul, making her feel small and unworthy. Toxic relationships had left their scars, and I desperately wanted to save her. But how could I?

All I ever wanted was for my parents to want me, to love me. As I grew older, God began to open my eyes, helping me understand that my parents loved me the best way they knew how. With this newfound understanding, I began to transform my pain into strength. As an adult, I made the decision to pour into them the love they had struggled to pour into me. I could not, and would not, give up on them.

I channeled my experiences into writing and singing, turning pain into purpose. My grandparents, recognizing my passion, encouraged me to pursue my dreams. They filled me with the belief that I could create a life rich in love and hope. Writing became my refuge, my voice. I penned stories of resilience, light breaking through the darkest clouds, and hope triumphing over despair. Each word I wrote was a testament to God's ability to turn pain into promise and sadness into joy.

Over time, I came to view my past not as a burden to carry, but as evidence of my strength. As I reflect on my journal entries, I offer a silent prayer of gratitude—for my grandparents, whose love enveloped me, and for the blessings that guided me through life's storms. I also pray for my parents, whom I love deeply. They are God's children too, and I know that with Him, all things are possible.

Isaiah 41:13

"For I the LORD thy God will hold thy right hand, saying unto thee, Fear not; I will help thee."
King James Version (KJV)

Chapter #16

GOD PUNCHES
Krissy

I never gave trauma enough credit. Sounds strange, doesn't it? I always thought trauma was something caused by someone else—an act with a clear perpetrator and victim. It was an event that had a cause and an effect. To me, trauma stemmed from death, violence, betrayal, or loss. And in my immature, self-absorbed way, I believed trauma only impacted people who allowed it to. Strong people, I thought, just brushed it off. That's exactly what I did—for 34 years.

My trauma wasn't from some catastrophic event; it was simply because I lived. I was five years old when my parents rushed me to the hospital with severe abdominal pain, vomiting, and fever. What followed was a whirlwind of 48 hours: being prepped for surgery that never happened, worsening symptoms, lethargy, and finally, an ambulance ride to a children's hospital two hours away.

There, the diagnosis hit—glomerulonephritis, a deadly kidney disease. My kidneys were functioning at only two percent. My feet were purple, my arms riddled with dead veins and raw skin from countless blood draws and IVs. My body was pumped with a dozen steroids daily, all in a desperate attempt to keep me alive. I was added to the transplant list. Nurses held me down—five of them—just to place an IV in my ankle, the only viable vein they could find. A week passed, symptoms worsened, and nothing seemed to work.

I was five. Two hours away from home. My parents never left my side, except for one gut-wrenching hour when doctors told them the prognosis wasn't good. My dad returned from that meeting, leaned over my hospital bed, and told me I had to fight. The family story goes that I punched him in the face. I don't remember that. What I do recall is a white rabbit named Leslie in the playroom I was wheeled to once a day and a 12-year-old boy lying in traction after a car accident. Even at five, I thought that was trauma. I was just sick.

The pep talk worked, and so did God. The next day, I started to improve. Two weeks later, I was released from the hospital, still swollen with steroids and scheduled for weekly doctor's visits. By the grace of God, I was cured. The doctors told my parents that if it didn't return before I turned nine, it likely wouldn't. I'm 39 now, and it hasn't. But I never processed it as trauma.

For 35 years, I carried on as though nothing had happened. The scar on my ankle was the only reminder of that experience, other than listing it in medical histories. That is, until I got pregnant with my miracle baby.

At 36, I thought the dream of having children had slipped away. I had stopped fighting for it, not realizing God already had a plan in motion. Through divine intervention, I met my husband. Initially, we didn't even speak—he was just there, helping his mother at a program I was coordinating. A year later, his mom passed away, and six months after her death, I met her son, my future husband.

He had three children and was upfront from the start that he couldn't have any more. I poured my heart into his kids, and we got engaged within five months. Overnight, I had the family I'd always dreamed of. But my heart ached for a child we could share together. After months of prayer and alignment with God's will, we decided to pursue IVF. We agreed that if God intended it, He would provide.

And He did. After countless shots and procedures, 16 eggs resulted in five embryos, and only one matured. Doctors told us the odds were slim: a 50% chance it was genetically normal and a 50% chance it would implant successfully. But in August 2023, the call came—I was officially pregnant.

Our joy was overwhelming, but by the fifth month, it was overshadowed by crippling anxiety. I had never experienced anxiety before. I prided myself on being a woman who had my shit together—damnit, but suddenly, I was unraveling. The devil exploited my vulnerability, dragging me back to the emotional state of my five-year-old self—not physically sick but spiritually ill.

Every symptom I googled convinced me something was wrong. My baby was dead inside me. I would give birth to a stillborn. I would die in labor. I didn't just think these things—I believed them. My past trauma resurfaced, magnifying my fears, and I was drowning in them.

My inability to regulate my emotions spiked my blood pressure. At 26 weeks, I was hospitalized with dangerously high readings. The OB told me we might have to deliver the baby early, with only a 15% chance of survival. My husband was my rock, singing silly songs during blood pressure checks, sleeping on hard hospital chairs, and doing everything to calm me. But nothing worked.

One night, he asked if I wanted him to pray with me. I said no. In my despair, I had turned my back on God and my husband—something I'd never done before. That night, I broke down, apologizing to God and begging for His direction and peace. The next morning, I asked my doctor for anxiety medication.

After ten grueling weeks of juggling two different anxiety medications, two blood pressure medications, hourly BP checks, light duty/bed rest, and profound soul-searching, we were finally scheduled for a C-section at 37 weeks. Those weeks were not just physically challenging—they were spiritually transformative. They brought me back to God in a way I desperately needed. It reminded me of when my dad told me I had to fight as a five-year-old battling kidney disease. Except this time, it wasn't my dad—I felt God telling me to fight. Instead of punching Him in the nose as a sign I understood, God punched me in the nose, making sure I truly heard Him. And I did.

On April 1, 2024, Kruze Jordan entered the world—six pounds, 12 ounces of God-made perfection. His first name, meaning "of the cross," felt like a divine message of the journey we had just endured. I vividly remember lying in the operating room, being stitched up after the C-section. My husband had been taken out of the room to do skin-to-skin with Kruze, and the doctors and nurses were busy finishing the procedure. For the first time, I found myself alone—arms stretched wide and tied down, mirroring the position of surrender. In that stillness, the enormity of what had just happened washed over me. Anxiety should have taken over, but instead, I felt an overwhelming peace, the greatest I've ever known in my 40 years of life. It was as if God Himself whispered, "We did it. Together, we conquered this."

When the nurses wheeled me into the post-op room, I was reunited with my incredible husband and our son. That moment was my own little slice of Heaven. Just the three of us, staring at each other in awe, while memories of my life played like a movie in the background. I saw the playroom at the children's hospital. I saw Leslie the bunny. And above all, I saw God's strength carrying me through it all.

Now, five months later, I know more joy and love than I ever imagined. I would do anything for this little guy. Being Kruze's mother is the greatest title I've ever held. And though I'm not spiritually where I want to be, I'm closer than ever, thanks to those **"God Punches."**

John 14:27

"Peace I leave with you, my peace I give unto you: not as the world giveth, give I unto you. Let not your heart be troubled, neither let it be afraid."

King James Version (KJV)

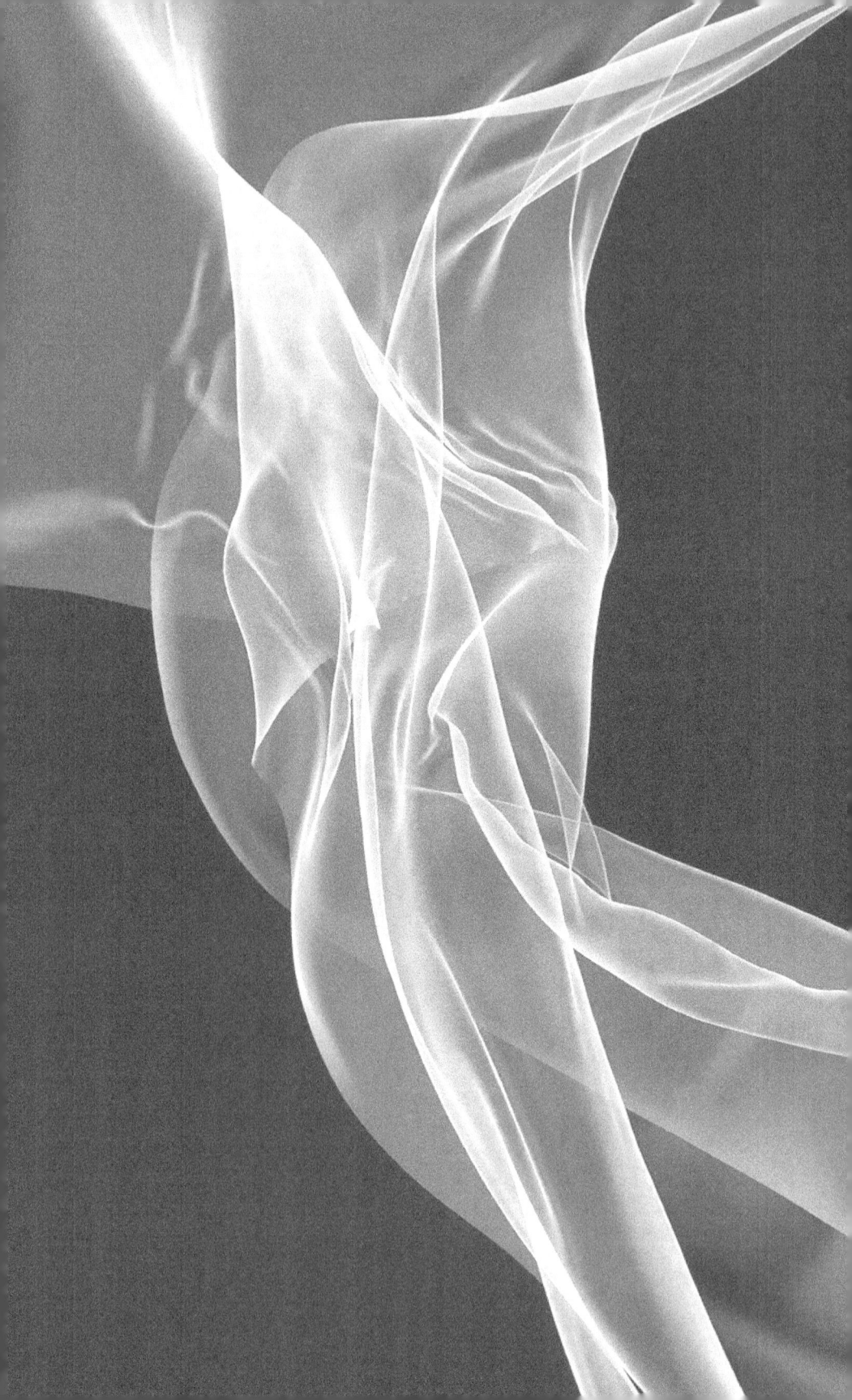

Chapter #17

REFLECTION AND PAIN
Janieka

It's hard to focus on just one trial in my life because my childhood was filled with so many. I am the product of a teenage mother who struggled with drug addiction and an alcoholic, abusive father. Whenever I reflect on my childhood, I feel a heavy drop in my stomach and a lump in my throat. It's not that I try to forget about it—how could I? The memories come with such vivid detail that they transport me right back into that pain.

One instance always lingers in the back of my mind. I can still see it clearly: my sisters and I being picked up from school by social workers. My mother had regained custody of us and had been doing well for months, but she fell back into her addiction. She hadn't been home in days. My oldest sister, just 12 years old and in the sixth grade, was the one finding food, getting us off to school, and doing her best to track down our mother after school. She confided in her friends—other kids her age—because who else could she turn to? Eventually, someone found out that our mother hadn't been home in nearly two weeks, and the social workers came for us.

This is the part that still makes me cry, that drags me back to that moment of fear, helplessness, and simultaneous pride. The three of us were taken to a foster home, and that's where we had to say goodbye to each other. We had been together all our lives—my sisters and I—and now, in that one defining moment, it was decided that we would be separated. The foster home would only take two of us, and they chose my older sisters to stay while I was sent to a different home.

At just 12 years old, my big sister refused to accept this. She flipped out. She was unyielding. Her little sisters were not going to be separated on her watch. Her defiance left no room for negotiation, and as a result, they sent her to a foster home alone. I still cry as an adult thinking about the weight of that decision. A child so young, forced to make a choice so profound, so selfless. My other sister and I were left, clinging to each other as our only source of comfort. That night, though we had bunk beds, we crawled into the same bed. Just like when we were little, she patted my back to soothe me and played with my ear to soothe herself.

The next day, we got up and faced the world. My sister did her best to do my hair, we switched outfits, and we went to school, where we were expected to perform as if nothing had changed. As if our sense of security hadn't been shattered. As if our big sister hadn't been taken. As if we didn't desperately want our mother to come home or to reach out to our Grammie.

I can't say that I've overcome this memory. Even at 41, it brings the same tears it did when I was 9. But I do know this: those painful parts of my childhood have shaped me into the determined mother I am today. I work tirelessly to parent my children to the best of my ability. I strive to always improve, to show them how deeply they are loved, and to remain consistent. That's my promise to them—and to myself.

Psalms 91:1

"He that dwelleth in the secret place of the most High shall abide under the shadow of the Almighty."
King James Version (KJV)

Chapter #18

NOBODY BUT GOD
Mary

In 1953, I was born in Selma, Alabama, a premature baby who spent the first six months of life in the hospital. My mother hailed from a small town about 50 miles outside Selma, and it was there that I grew up, experiencing a chaotic childhood, to say the least. My father was absent, but thank God for my grandfather and uncles, who stepped in as father figures.

At an early age, I became aware that my mother had a drinking problem. Alcohol consumed her every day, and as I grew older, her dependency worsened. As a child, I believed it was my fault. I thought if I were good enough, helpful enough, maybe she'd stop. But no matter what I did, she drank. And drank. And drank.

My mother, my siblings, and I lived with my grandparents, along with some of my cousins. The household could be toxic. My grandmother's verbally abusive words cut deep, stripping away what little self-worth I had. Amid this turmoil, my mother decided to leave the small Alabama town and move to New York, dreaming of a fresh start. Little did I know, her plans didn't include me or my brother. She packed her bags and left us behind. After she was gone, my grandmother's verbal abuse only intensified.

When my mother returned from New York, she wasn't alone. She came back with a baby—my baby sister, Kim. There were now three of us, and over time, two more siblings joined our family. As the eldest, I was tasked with taking care of my younger siblings. When my mother moved us to Birmingham, Alabama, I remember being sent home from school when President Kennedy was assassinated. The following year, I lived in fear after the 16th Street Baptist Church bombing, just down the street from our home. Those events cemented my desire to leave Alabama.

As my mother's drinking spiraled out of control, she often left me alone with my siblings while she went on binges that lasted days, sometimes a week. We were left to fend for ourselves. Thank God we had family in Bessemer, Alabama, who stepped in to help when they could because they knew our difficult circumstances. By age 10, I had endured unimaginable pain, often falling victim to sexual abuse, molested by my cousin, and rape by both my mother's boyfriends. The confusion and hurt were overwhelming for a young girl.

At 11 or 12, we moved back to the country with my grandparents. Life there added another layer of trauma—verbal and physical abuse. My grandmother told me I would never amount to anything and should have died before I was born. I internalized her words, believing something was wrong with me and if was all my fault, or so I thought. I dreamed of escaping and even tried running away, but I was not successful.

With my mother's alcoholism as a constant shadow, mistreatment became our norm. I was the oldest, so I bore the brunt of the abuse, though my brother Marvin endured his share as well. I wanted to protect my siblings, to make things better, but I didn't know how. I blamed my mother, and the pain and anger consumed me.

Still, no daddy. I felt utterly alone. My heart ached with the emptiness of not being cared for or loved. That void led me to make poor choices. In 1968, I began spending my summers in Chicago with my aunt and uncles. In the fall of 1971, I was arrested during a protest against segregation and spent three days in jail. Afterward, my mother finally gave me permission to move to Chicago. In 1972, I left Alabama for good, determined to carve out a new life for myself.

In Chicago, I finished high school and later in the fall of 1973, I attended Kentucky State University. College was intimidating at first with no family nearby, but I made three lifelong friends on my first day. I also met my college sweetheart. For the first time, I felt truly cared for. Still, college had its lonely moments. My heart broke when no one from my family visited or attended my graduation. Watching my peers celebrate with their families while I stood alone was devastating. That day, I vowed to rely only on myself.

After graduation, I returned to Chicago and began working for Montgomery Ward. The company eventually transferred me to Fort Wayne, Indiana, for training. The move was long and lonely. In 1979, I became a mother. The pregnancy wasn't planned, but I now know it was part of God's plan. As a single mother living far from family, God surrounded me with individuals who became my support system.

In 1983, I reconnected with my college sweetheart, and we married. I was on top of the world. Our second son was born in 1984, but four years later, my husband left us. Once again, I found myself a single mother, now raising two boys on my own. The struggle was overwhelming, but God carried us through.

Raising boys into men as a single mother is no easy task, but God blessed me with two incredible sons who stayed away from trouble, gangs, and drugs. I remain deeply grateful for the village of people God placed in our lives to help guide us.

In 1991, at age 38, I finally met my father. My sister on my mother's side helped me find him. While I was happy to meet him, I was also angry. He had known about me but never made an effort to be part of my life. I discovered I had five more sisters and another brother who had grown up just an hour away from me. My father died in 2000, and I never got the heart-to-heart father-daughter talk I longed for, I treasure the connection I have with my siblings. I don't see them much, but when I go back home to Alabama, I check in on them.

It has taken years, but I've come to understand that everything I went through shaped me into the person I am today. Life hasn't been perfect, but God has been faithful. While I may never fully heal from the neglect, abuse, and disappointment of my past, I know that God has kept me.

The scars remain, and triggers still arise, but I hold tightly to my faith. **But God**—nobody but God—has carried me through it all. For that, I am eternally grateful.

Psalms 23:1

"The LORD *is* my shepherd; I shall not want."
King James Version (KJV)

Chapter #19

HIDING BEHIND FAKE SMILES, FAKE HAPPINESS, FAKE LIFE

Rachel

Hiding behind fake smiles to the crowd, in hopes of not being discovered—
Discovered that the strength perceived by onlookers is as thin as a butterfly's wing,
Allowing hope to escape out the open window of her heart,
Where love and trust once lay.

Black eyes, bruised arms, and a wounded soul are what love taps leave behind.
Down on her knees, but not in prayer, she cries,
"Who am I to ask God for help, when I won't even help me?"

Hiding behind fake happiness so her children wake up never having to know that pain—
Pain that stretches further than her memory of life before it,
Yet is felt as easily as the breeze that blows through her unkempt hair.

You see, beauty invites his rage, so it's ugliness she must choose.
But being ugly comes with its own price, and the payment is no longer fair.
His venomous lips spew words that leave her damaged
Long before the first blow ever strikes her face.

Hiding behind a fake life—
Thinking she can change a man who has spent a lifetime creating

himself.
A fake life, pretending all is well,
Because the tapestry of colors, with each changing bruise,
Is the only real evidence of a new beginning.

The eyes of her children have witnessed what they cannot understand,
But will grow to become.

So today, this is her—
Coming out of hiding.

Hebrews 11:1

"Now faith is the substance of things hoped for, the evidence of
things not seen."
King James Version (KJV)

Chapter #20

<u>SEARCHING FOR HOME</u>
Nita

I sat in the coffee shop, my heart caught between hope and trepidation. The aroma of freshly brewed coffee filled the air, but today my heart felt heavy with memories. As I sipped on my coffee and nibbled on my bagel, a realization struck me: each man I had dated over the years had been a fleeting escape, a placeholder in my search for something I had yet to define. But deep down, I knew the truth. What I was really searching for was the father I never had. Sounds crazy, huh? Well, it's a fact.

Growing up, my father was a phantom—a fleeting presence that materialized for scattered weekends, holidays, or the occasional week during summer breaks. His absence echoed loudly through the hallways of my childhood. In his place, I filled the void with boyfriends, hoping to find in them the love, security, and affirmation I so deeply craved. They were charming and sweet, but ultimately, they were shadows— poor imitations of the father figure I longed for.

As the years passed, my search for love took me down many misguided paths. There was the charismatic guy who dazzled me, only to disappear when he realized I wouldn't tolerate his disrespect. Then came the smooth-talker who whispered sweet nothings, but his words turned out to be hollow, his attention scattered among countless other women. Each failed relationship left me feeling emptier, the void in my heart growing wider and deeper.

One evening, as tears streamed down my face, I found myself laying my head in my grandmother's lap. Her gentle hand stroked my hair as she reminded me, "There is no greater love than the love of God." Her words settled in my spirit, and the following Sunday, I found myself sitting in church. The pastor spoke about love—not the kind found in fleeting human connections, but the enduring love that comes from God. His words pierced my heart, stirring a realization I had long avoided. As tears welled in my eyes, I silently thanked God for sending me the confirmation I didn't even know I needed.

The love I had been desperately seeking wasn't to be found in the arms of a man—it had always been in the comforting presence of my heavenly Father. It was a love that required no conditions, no performance, and no validation from anyone else.

While I had grown up in the church, I knew in my heart that I needed and wanted to rededicate my life to God. With each service, I felt myself being drawn closer to Him, each sermon pulling me deeper into the vastness of His love. As I walked this new path, I began to release the anger and disappointment I had carried for so long toward my biological father. I realized he may never have been equipped to be the father I needed, but I had a heavenly Father who had always been there, loving me with a profound, perfect love.

Months later, I found myself back in the same coffee shop where I had once sat, longing for love and drowning in loneliness. But this time, my heart was different. I wasn't dwelling on my past or chasing after something unattainable. Instead, I was celebrating the love I had discovered within myself and in my faith.

As I sipped my coffee, a soft smile spread across my face, and I even let out a giggle. God was turning things around in my favor. Self-love, once so elusive, was now within my reach.

At that moment, I understood what I had been missing all along: true love isn't about finding a father figure or a romantic partner. It's about embracing the unwavering love that God freely offers and learning to love yourself through His eyes. With this realization, I finally felt whole, ready to face the world with a heart full of hope and a soul anchored in peace.

No, life didn't become perfect overnight, but it became complete. Complete with the unshakable love I found in God—the love that filled every gap, soothed every wound, and gave me the strength to love myself fully.

Psalms 25:16

"Turn thee unto me, and have mercy upon me; for I *am* desolate and afflicted."
King James Version (KJV)

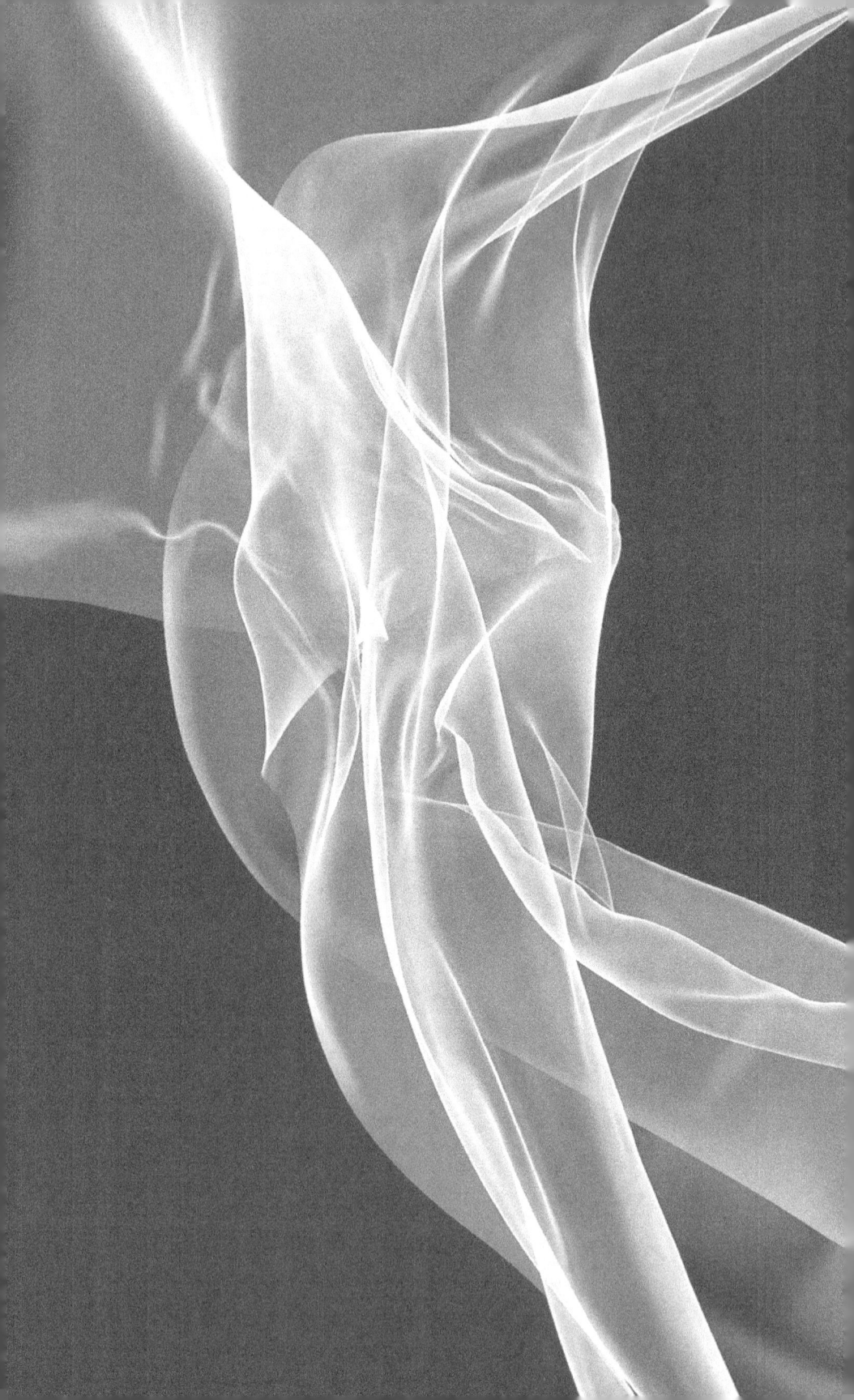

Chapter #21

<u>FINDING STRENGTH IN HEARTBREAK</u>
Anonymous

My husband and I were the picture of a good Christian couple—or so I believed. We shared dreams, laughter, and a connection that seemed unbreakable. For years, we built a life filled with love and companionship. I embraced his extended family, and he embraced mine. Our lives intertwined seamlessly, and I felt secure in the future we were creating. But then, one day, everything changed.

Returning home earlier than expected, I walked into our house and into the bedroom—only to find my husband with another man. The shock and anger hit me like a freight train, shattering my entire world. In that moment, love turned to betrayal, and the life I thought I knew crumbled before me. Everything I believed about my marriage, my husband, and even myself became a dark shadow and a painful lie.

The aftermath was devastating. I felt consumed by waves of emotion—anger, confusion, humiliation, and profound sadness. It was as if the ground beneath me had disappeared, leaving me to free-fall into an abyss of uncertainty. The love I had nurtured for so many years felt like a distant, mocking memory, replaced by the cold sting of betrayal. Days became nights, and nights became endless stretches of tears, sleeplessness, and a broken heart I wasn't sure could ever be repaired.

As the reality of the situation set in, I faced the agonizing decision to end my marriage. Divorce wasn't just a legal process; it was the severing of dreams, hopes, and the future I had envisioned. Saying goodbye to my husband wasn't the hardest part—letting go of the life we had built together was. I mourned the loss of what could have been, grieving not only the relationship but also the woman I had been within it.

In my darkest hours, I turned to my faith. Raised in a loving household that placed great importance on spirituality, I sought solace in prayer and scripture. I clung to verses that spoke of hope, healing, and the promise of a new day. Slowly, through those moments of reflection, I realized I was not alone. The Lord's presence wrapped around me like a comforting embrace, reminding me that my worth was not tied to someone else's choices.

I started attending church more regularly, joined support groups, and immersed myself in a community that uplifted me. I leaned on the words of others who had endured heartbreak, finding strength in their stories as I began to rebuild my own.

Starting over wasn't easy. A new home, a new mindset, a new version of myself—I had to create it all from the ground up. The path was full of ups and downs, and there were days when the pain felt insurmountable. But leaning on God, I learned to navigate those tumultuous waters. I began journaling, pouring my heart onto the pages as I documented my journey from despair to hope. Writing became my sanctuary, an outlet to process my emotions and uncover the strength buried within me.

As time passed, I began to reclaim my identity. I explored new hobbies, reconnected with old friends, and allowed myself the grace to rediscover who I was outside of my marriage. Each small step forward was a victory, a reminder of my resilience and my ability to rise above the hurt.

Years later, I now stand as a testament to the power of healing and faith. The scars of betrayal remain, but they've been transformed into symbols of strength rather than reminders of pain. I share my story openly, hoping to inspire others who have experienced similar heartache. While my marriage ended, my capacity to love especially to love myself—has grown beyond measure.

In the midst of heartbreak, I found strength. And in finding strength, I found myself.

Psalms 55:22

"Cast thy burden upon the LORD, and he shall sustain thee: he shall never suffer the righteous to be moved."
King James Version (KJV)

Chapter #22

THE GIFT OF STRENGTH
Cheri

My story begins a long time ago, with some of my earliest memories—sadly, memories of my parents' divorce and the day my dad left. I was five years old, clinging to his leg, begging him not to go. I can still picture his outfit as if it were yesterday: white shorts and a blue-and-white seersucker shirt. He tried, in some vague way, to console me, but he left all the same.

Shortly after, my mother remarried, and looking back, I realize that's when the chaos began. I was too young to understand what was happening, but within a few short years, our newly blended family—including my two older brothers—began moving around. We left Ohio and eventually settled in Illinois for several years. As the youngest and the only girl, I often played by myself at home. Something—perhaps an angel watching over me—guided me to stay in my room, away from the yelling and screaming that filled our house. I didn't know it then, but physical abuse was also a constant presence in our home, affecting my mother and brothers.

Then, seemingly overnight, my oldest brother left to live with my father. My mother was devastated, and I was left with another core memory of loss.

Shortly after that, my mother, stepfather, middle brother, and I moved back to Ohio. I was in fourth grade then, and the chaos only escalated. Although I was mostly spared from physical abuse, I couldn't avoid witnessing it. I remember one horrifying incident when my stepfather struck my mother on the head with a phone receiver, knocking her unconscious. My middle brother, a teenager with a chip on his shoulder, became an easy target for my stepfather, a severe functioning alcoholic.

The next few years are a blur. I can only imagine what could have happened to me during that time and how it might have shaped the rest of my life. What I do remember is that things got so bad my mother sent me to stay with my grandmother for an entire summer. At the time, I thought it was because she lived on a farm, and it would be fun. Looking back, I realize it was likely to protect me.

My father was absent for most of this turmoil. He had moved on with his life, remarried, and focused on his new family. Even though my oldest brother lived with him, my father showed himself to be the selfish man we would come to know throughout our lives. When my middle brother reached out to him for help, showing clear signs of abuse, my father turned a blind eye.

Despite her petite frame—barely five feet tall, as she liked to joke—my mother eventually found the strength to leave the abusive relationship. I can't say for sure why she left. Was it to protect her children? To save herself? All I know is that she was broken and sad, her heart shattered by a man she had loved deeply after a divorce from my father, who had never been present. Despite her strength in leaving, depression began to take hold. At the time, I was too young to understand it, and all I saw was my mom—my favorite person, my best friend, and my partner in errands and shopping adventures.

After we left my stepfather, my mother, brother, and I moved into an apartment. My brother had turned to his friends for solace and was rarely around. When he was, there was constant fighting between him and my mother. Soon after, my mother accepted a job in another state, and my brother chose to live with my father to stay close to his friends, who had become his chosen family. My mother and I moved away, leaving me to grapple with yet another core memory of loss.

During the chaos, my mother and I had been incredibly close. She didn't speak much about what was happening at home, but she embodied the perfect mother to her little girl. When it was just the two of us, our bond deepened. I learned about her younger years, her own childhood struggles, and the cycles of abuse and dysfunction that had shaped her life.

Youth has a way of granting innocence, allowing you to accept things as "just the way they are." For me, that innocence began to fade as I grew older and understood the dynamics at play. I developed a forgiving heart, recognizing that people are often shaped by their circumstances. My mother's life had been marked by hardship, rejection, and heartbreak, much of which she carried silently.

Tragically, her struggles overwhelmed her. In November of 1984, my mother ended her life. She was just 42 years old, and I was a few weeks shy of my 16th birthday.

Her death changed my life in an instant. In the six days she was on life support, I had to grow up fast—making calls to my brothers, listening to medical conversations I barely understood, and preparing myself for the inevitable. I remember holding her tiny hand in the ICU, telling her how much I loved her and begging her to come home. I whispered the lyrics to our song, *"You and Me Against the World"* by Helen Reddy, and her hand squeezed mine. Or at least, I chose to believe it did.

When she passed, I moved into survival mode. I justified her decision, holding no anger—only sadness. I believed she had fought for happiness and that this was her way of finding peace.

The years that followed were a series of challenges no teenager should face. Miraculously, a teacher at my high school and his family took me in, allowing me to stay in familiar surroundings and graduate with my friends. It was a gift I am eternally grateful for, even though I now see the need for the counseling I never received at that critical time.

Life went on, and so did I. I attended Ohio State University, lived with my father briefly, and built a life for myself. Eventually, I met my husband and had two beautiful daughters. Life was not without its struggles, but I carried my mother's strength with me. When my oldest daughter faced medical challenges as a baby, I leaned on that strength, though I missed my mother more than ever.

Through heartbreak, loss, and adversity, I've learned that strength is not the absence of struggle but the ability to rise despite it. My mother's life, though filled with pain, left me with the greatest gift: the strength to face life head-on and to choose love, forgiveness, and forward motion.

To my grandparents, who were my safe haven, and to my mother, who fought so hard, I thank you. Your resilience lives on in me. It is because of you that I know how to navigate life's storms and cherish its blessings.

Deuteronomy 31:6

"Be strong and of a good courage, fear not, nor be afraid of them: for the LORD thy God, he *it is* that doth go with thee; he will not fail thee, nor forsake thee."

King James Version (KJV)

Chapter #23

<u>EVER FORWARD</u>
Kizmet

My life once felt like an endless cycle of trauma—sadness, anxiety, and despair interwoven into the fabric of my existence. Depression weighed heavily on my mental health, dragging me down until I hit rock bottom. I was isolated, frustrated, and scared, carrying the burdens of childhood pain into my adult life. My world was in shambles.

One day, something shifted. I confronted the pain head-on, tired of the numbness that had consumed me for so long. It was then that I realized I was worthy of a happy life. I sought help, taking the first tentative steps toward healing. I started with my primary care doctor, who referred me to a psychiatrist. That's when I received a diagnosis: major depressive disorder and generalized anxiety.

Hearing those words left me breathless. I was flooded with questions: *How could this be? What do I do now? Who can I tell?* The diagnosis unleashed a constant cycle of fear—fear that I might never get better, fear of the stigma, fear of facing this reality.

Then therapy happened.

Therapy became a safe space—a sanctuary where I could talk, cry, and be vulnerable. I went through a rollercoaster of emotions, and there were times I walked out of those sessions feeling ashamed. But I kept showing up. Months passed, and my treatment began to take shape.

New medications were prescribed to manage my symptoms, and I gradually began to feel a sense of balance.

In time, therapy became my comfort. I opened up, peeling back the layers of pain that had held me captive for so long. That's when I discovered EMDR (Eye Movement Desensitization and Reprocessing) therapy—a powerful technique that helped me process the childhood trauma I had carried like a heavy shadow. Through this treatment, I began to move forward, reclaiming my life with a renewed sense of clarity and hope.

Amid my healing journey, I turned to prayer, asking for courage and discipline to see me through. Slowly but surely, I started to rise— like a phoenix emerging from the ashes. Strength and clarity became my companions as I moved ever forward.

Today, my life is full of joy.

I laugh freely. I sing loudly. I cook meals that fill my home with warmth and laughter. I cherish the company of my family and friends. Through faith, grace, and determination, I've found a life worth living.

I am no longer on medication for depression or anxiety—a gradual and thoughtful process I worked through with my doctors. While there are still hard moments, I now meet them with prayer, meditation, exercise, and, most importantly, self-love.

My feet are firmly planted in the belief that I am deserving of all good things. The journey hasn't been easy, but it has been transformative. I've learned to embrace life with open arms, trusting in my resilience and the power of moving ever forward.

Psalms 55:22

"Cast thy burden upon the LORD, and he shall sustain thee: he shall never suffer the righteous to be moved."

King James Version (KJV)

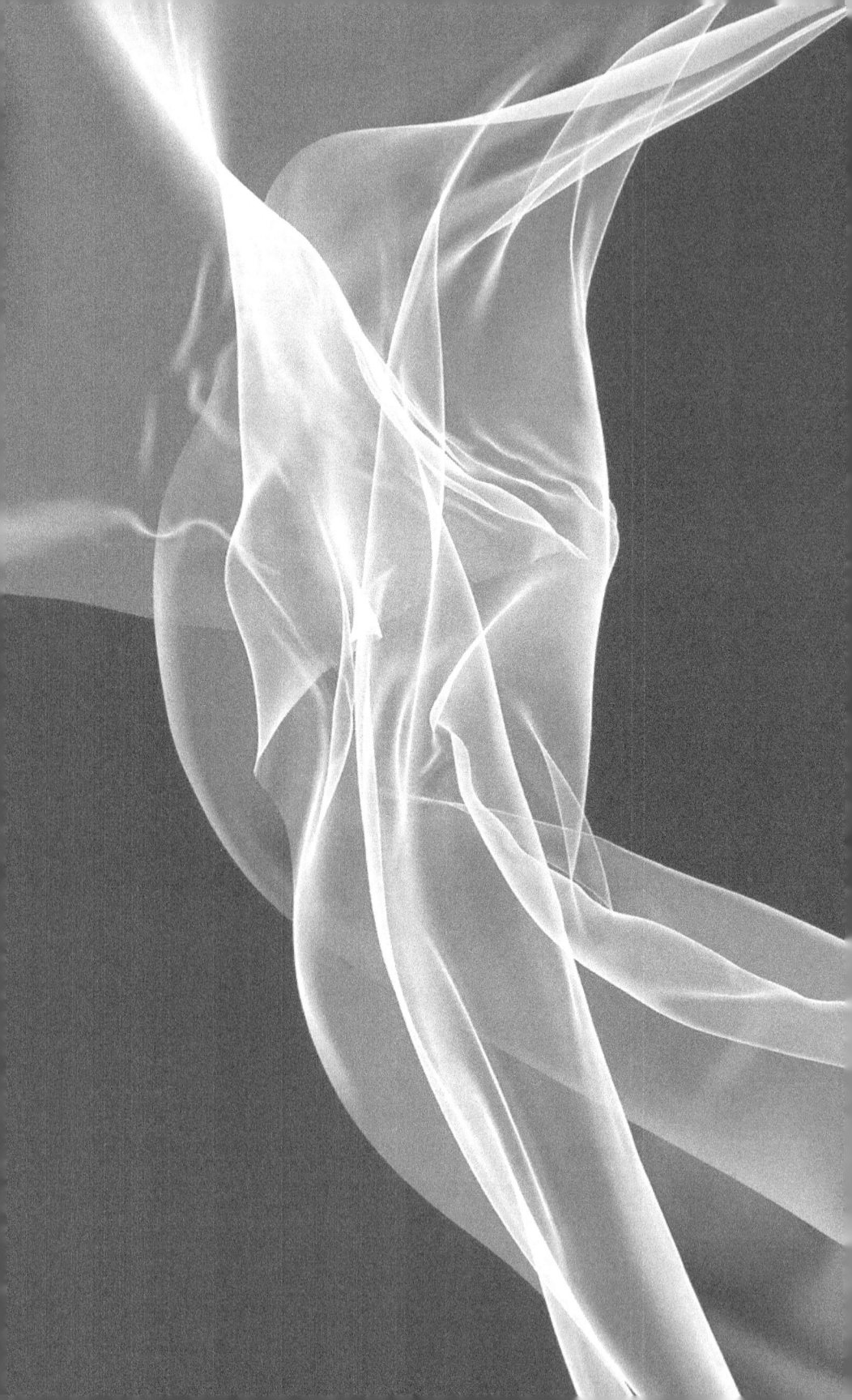

Chapter #24

GOD, I WILL FOREVER TRUST YOU
Sireana

The Crossroads of Life

In Chapter 24 of my life, I faced challenges that felt like unrelenting storms. Every day was a battle, and I often found myself questioning God, whispering "Why?" through tearful prayers. Why was life so difficult? Why did I feel so lost and confused?

I had always imagined a life filled with purpose and love, yet I felt untethered. Without direction, I struggled with self-acceptance and self-worth. It was as if I were moving through life without truly living it, burdened by a deep ache of misunderstanding—not just from others, but from within myself.

Despite these struggles, time moved forward. Eventually, I set a goal: to live intentionally. It wasn't a grand vision but a commitment to take charge of my life, refusing to let circumstances dictate my happiness. That resolve was tested when I became a single mother.

The Unexpected Journey

Becoming a single mother was never part of my plan. I envisioned a life where I would achieve my dreams with a loving partner by my side. Instead, I found myself raising my first child alone. It was a daunting responsibility that left me feeling overwhelmed and uncertain.

In my solitude, I turned to God with fervent prayers, asking Him to send me someone who could complement my life and share in the love I held for Him. I prayed not just for a partner, but for a connection that reflected my values and faith.

But before I could welcome someone else into my life, I had to learn to love myself. That lesson was transformative. Embracing self-love meant recognizing my worth and setting boundaries for how I should be treated. It gave me the strength to seek out a partner who truly deserved me.

Meeting My Loving Husband

When I met Monte, my prayers began to take shape. A former Navy man who had served for eight years, he embodied strength and dedication. Standing 6'1" with hazel eyes that sometimes shifted to green, he carried a quiet compassion that captivated me.

Our connection was immediate and profound. We fell deeply in love, and before long, we married and blended our lives. Monte had a bonus son, and together we had five sons. Our family of six energetic boys was full of life, laughter, and love.

I remembered my prayers and marveled at how God had answered them. Monte was everything I had asked for—and more. Our love story was proof of the power of faith and the beauty of waiting for God's perfect timing.

The Trials of Love

Our love, though strong, was not without challenges. Love is a journey, it requires patience, growth, and understanding. One of the hardest trials we faced was Monte's struggle with post-traumatic stress disorder (PTSD). His experiences in the Navy left emotional scars that deeply affected him and, in turn, our family.

PTSD tested us in ways I never expected. I often felt overwhelmed, questioning my ability to provide the support he needed. But through it all, I leaned on my faith. I believed God had placed me in Monte's life for a reason, even when the path was difficult to see.

Growing Through the Storm

Supporting Monte through PTSD was one of the most transformative experiences of my life. It taught me patience, resilience, and how to lean on God for strength. My prayers became my anchor, and scripture provided a guiding light in the darkest moments.

The journey was painful but enlightening. It deepened my relationship with God and strengthened my understanding of love and commitment. Monte and I grew together through the storms, and our bond became a testament to the power of faith.

The Final Chapter

At age 37, I faced the unimaginable: the loss of my loving husband. It was not part of my dream, but it was part of God's greater plan. The grief was overwhelming, yet I clung to my faith, whispering, "God, I trust You," even as my heart ached with loss.

Through the pain, I held onto the lessons Monte and I had learned together. I trusted that God's purpose, though hard to understand, was unfolding as it should. My love for Monte remains, but my faith in God sustains me.

Moving Forward with Faith

As I continue to move forward, my heart is full of faith and unwavering trust in God. The journey has been long and fraught with challenges, but it has also been one of profound growth and deeper understanding. I have learned to trust in God's plan, even when it deviates from my own dreams and expectations.

My story is a testament to the transformative power of faith and the importance of trusting God through every chapter of life. Each obstacle and trial has strengthened my belief in His infinite wisdom and love. I now understand that even in the most difficult times, God is quietly and purposefully guiding us toward a greater destiny.

I hold tightly to the promise that God's plan is always perfect, even when it isn't immediately clear. This journey has revealed to me that trusting in God is not merely a passive belief but an active, deliberate commitment to surrendering my will to His. It is a path of faith, love, and perseverance, and I am deeply grateful for every step along the way.

Living Life Like a Sunflower

At the age of 38, as the sun dipped below the horizon, painting the sky in hues of gold and orange, I stood in my garden with a smile spreading across my face. The sunflowers, tall and vibrant, reached toward the heavens with quiet yet resolute strength. Their unwavering posture, always turned toward the light, inspired me deeply.

In many ways, I saw myself in those sunflowers. My journey had been a tapestry of trials and triumphs, moments of doubt intertwined with flashes of clarity. Through it all, I had learned to stand firm, deeply rooted in faith and grounded by God's promises. Like those sunflowers that bend but never break, I, too, had learned to remain steadfast, to keep my faith unshaken, and to continually turn toward the light of God's word.

There were days when the storms of life seemed relentless—when the winds howled, and the rain poured down without mercy. Yet, just as the sunflowers endured the harsh elements, I found strength and refuge in God's word. His promises became my shelter, my guide, and my source of nourishment. Like the warm rays of the sun, His word nurtured my spirit and helped me to bloom where I was planted.

Taking a deep breath, I let the serenity of the moment wash over me. My heart overflowed with gratitude for the victories, both great and small, that had marked my path. Each victory, no matter how seemingly insignificant, was a testament to God's grace and steadfast love—a reminder of His unending faithfulness.

As I whispered a prayer of thanks, I recognized that my life's journey was a living testament to the power of faith. I had learned to trust in the unseen and to believe in promises even when the way forward was unclear. In that trust, I found a peace so profound it felt unshakable.

Standing in the glow of the setting sun, I marveled at the beauty that had blossomed in my life. The sunflowers, with their golden petals and towering presence, were symbols of the strength and resilience I aspired to embody every day. They reminded me of the unwavering faith that had carried me through life's challenges.

With a heart full of praise and thanksgiving, I resolved to continue standing strong in God's promises. I would strive to keep my faith as vibrant and steadfast as the sunflowers in my garden, cherishing every victory along the way. Each day, I would aim to live like a sunflower—strong, resilient, and ever-reaching toward the divine light that guides and sustains me.

And so, with gratitude in my heart and faith as my compass, I embraced the journey ahead. I felt ready to face whatever challenges lay before me with the same resilience and hope that had brought me this far. Like the sunflowers, I knew I would continue to grow and thrive, nourished always by the boundless love and grace of God.

Prayer of Gratitude and Strength

Heavenly Father,

As I come before You, my heart overflows with gratitude and awe for the countless blessings You have poured into my life. Thank You for guiding me through the highs and the lows, for the victories that shine brightly as reminders of Your grace and unwavering faithfulness.

Lord, I am inspired by the sunflowers in my garden, standing tall and steadfast despite the trials they endure. Help me to mirror their strength and resilience in my own life. Teach me to remain grounded in faith, keeping my eyes fixed on Your light, even when the path ahead is uncertain. Let Your word be my guiding sun, warming and nurturing my spirit with every step I take.

I praise You for the victories, both great and small, that have shaped my journey. Each one is a testament to Your boundless love and unfailing support. I humbly ask that You continue to bless me with courage and strength to face each new day with unwavering faith. May I always find comfort in Your promises and peace in Your presence.

Grant me the wisdom to see Your hand at work in every moment, and the grace to respond with a heart full of thankfulness and joy. Help me to stand firm in Your word, living a life that reflects Your love and mercy, and shining as a beacon of Your light to others. As I move forward, let Your Spirit be my guide, Your love my strength, and Your grace my foundation.

I place my trust in You, Lord, knowing that You are with me every step of the way. Thank You for being my anchor in the storm, my refuge in times of need, and my light in the darkness.

With a heart full of praise and gratitude, I lift this prayer to You. May my life flourish like the sunflowers in Your garden, always reaching toward Your divine light and reflecting Your endless love.

In Jesus' name,
Amen.

Psalms 34:18

"The LORD *is* nigh unto them that are of a broken heart; and saveth such as be of a contrite spirit."
King James Version (KJV)

Chapter #25

MIRACLE OF MOTHERHOOD
Nita

I sat in the sterile examination room, my heart heavy with the weight of the doctor's words. His tone was detached, clinical, as he explained that my cervical opening was too small for conception. The words cut deep, piercing through my sense of womanhood. Tears streamed down my face as despair threatened to overwhelm me. But in that moment of pain, a flicker of hope ignited within me. I wiped my tears, looked the doctor square in the eye, and declared with unshakable conviction, "I serve a God who performs miracles, and I know He can do the same for me."

The doctor's skeptical expression only deepened, but his disbelief couldn't shake my faith. Every biblical lesson I had learned as a child and the faith that had carried me through life now demanded action.

As I left the doctor's office, I felt an odd mix of trauma and empowerment. The weight of his words lingered, but so did the promise of God's power. Once home, I fell to my knees, tears pouring as I prayed with a fervor I had never known. I laid my heart bare before God, pleading for the miracle I so deeply desired.

Weeks passed, and one morning, I noticed something was different. My menstrual cycle had not arrived. A surge of both panic and hope gripped me as I rushed to the store, my hands trembling as I grabbed a pregnancy test. Back at home, my heart raced as I followed the instructions on the box. I held the test in my hands, willing it to reveal the answer to my prayers. Within seconds, two bold lines appeared.

Joy erupted from my lips as I screamed and ran through the house, tears streaming down my face. "God has done it! He has performed a miracle!" I cried, my voice full of wonder and gratitude.

Grabbing my phone, I dialed my husband. "Hey, Daddy!" I exclaimed, my voice trembling with excitement. "What are you talking about?" he asked, confusion clear in his tone. But as my words sank in, realization dawned. "Are you serious?" he asked, his voice thick with emotion. "Yes!" I squealed, "I'm pregnant!" His disbelief turned into tears, and together, we celebrated the miraculous news.

Two weeks later, my husband and I returned to the doctor's office for confirmation. Sitting in the examination room, I felt nervous but confident. When the doctor entered, he greeted me casually, "How are you today, Shenita?" With a triumphant smile, I replied, "I'm great! I'm pregnant!"

His expression shifted, skepticism creeping back into his eyes. "Don't get too excited," he cautioned. "I told you this wasn't possible." I met his gaze, unshaken. "Doctor, please do the tests and examination. I know God performed a miracle."

The nurse drew my blood, and the doctor prepared for a physical examination. Turning to my husband with a chuckle, he said, "Man, you must have had a golden bullet. Your wife is pregnant."

Shaking my head with a smile, I replied, "No, my God provided us with a golden miracle. There is nothing too hard for the God I serve!"

Laughter and tears filled the room as my husband and I embraced, overwhelmed by the confirmation of God's goodness. The pregnancy journey wasn't easy; there were moments of fear and uncertainty, but through it all, God was faithful. We were blessed to welcome our daughter, Chaslyn, into the world—a living testament to the miraculous power of faith.

As I cradled my daughter in my arms for the first time, I whispered a prayer of gratitude. This journey had not only changed my life but deepened my faith in a God who answers prayers in the most extraordinary ways. Chaslyn is my reminder that with God, all things are possible.

Hebrews 11:6

"But without faith it is impossible to please him: for he that cometh to God must believe that he is, and that he is a rewarder of them that diligently seek him."
King James Version (KJV)

Chapter #26

IN THE MIDST OF IT ALL
Allison

I never thought that six months after graduating high school, my life would take such a drastic turn. But it did. I was a freshman in college, eager to further my education and chase my dreams. What I thought was just a common cold turned into something far worse.

My college was an hour away from my hometown, and as my cold worsened, my mom urged me to come home to see a doctor. What happened next changed everything. I ended up in the hospital, and life became a blur. I spent 12 ½ weeks in a medically induced coma, surrounded by countless tubes and machines. My family and friends have shared stories about those weeks, but I have little memory of it all. Doctors ran test after test, searching for answers to the health crisis that had taken over my body.

The moment I opened my eyes, I remember seeing my friend and my mom by my side. I had no idea what had happened. That was in 2005. Afterward, I spent 6 ½ months in hospitals, slowly being nursed back to health. When I finally returned home, life as I knew it was gone.

I was now a 19-year-old in a wheelchair, doing physical therapy, relearning basic tasks like eating. I felt as though my life had been stripped away. Eventually, I learned that I had contracted viral encephalitis—an inflammation of the brain caused by a virus. The most serious potential complication is permanent brain damage. To this day, the doctors do not know how I contracted it or how to cure it.

In 2007, they came up with a secondary diagnosis: multiple sclerosis (MS), a chronic disease that affects the central nervous system, including the brain, spinal cord, and optic nerves. But even this diagnosis felt uncertain, like an educated guess. It was frustrating. It still is. To this day, they don't have clear answers, but I know who holds the answers—Jesus Christ.

I was raised in the church, a young woman of faith. But I'll be honest: I was angry with God. Why did this happen to me? What did I do to deserve this? In the blink of an eye, my life—and my family's life—was flipped upside down. My emotions became a rollercoaster, full of unexpected twists and turns. I cried more tears than I knew were inside of me.

Initially, I didn't even think about the trauma because I was just grateful to be alive. But as time passed, I realized that what I had endured was deeply traumatic. I missed out on so many things that others take for granted. I couldn't just hop in my car to meet friends or take spontaneous trips. I struggled to imagine having a meaningful relationship with a man because I felt vulnerable, and I feared that men only saw that vulnerability as something to exploit.

Now, at 37 years old, I have come to realize that I didn't do anything wrong. God's plan for my life wasn't punishment; it was preparation. He wanted to use my story to bring glory to His name, to show the world that miracles still happen.

In the midst of it all, I never lost faith. Through brain bleeds, respiratory failure, and countless other odds stacked against me, I have survived. When the doctors said no, God said yes. I am living proof of His miracles.

God told me that He would use my life to touch others, to share His goodness and grace. He's opened doors for me to share my testimony, and through that, I've learned the power of surrender. I once read that disbelief disrupts our destiny. It's true. When we hold back from giving God our whole selves, we block the miracles He has for us.

No matter what you're going through, I encourage you to surrender it all to God. In the midst of your pain, your confusion, your struggles—He is there. I am living proof that even in the hardest times, God's grace prevails. Give Him your all and watch Him work miracles in your life.

Jeremiah 17:14

"Heal me, O LORD, and I shall be healed; save me, and I shall be saved: for thou art my praise."
King James Version (KJV)

Chapter #27

SHE DESTROYED LIVES
Anonymous

I HATED HER! From the moment she entered the world, I knew her, but I could never truly understand her. Even as a young girl, she craved excitement and validation, as if she were trying to fill a void too vast to ever be satisfied. Everyone who knew her could see it—she had a dangerous addiction to sex and drugs. She spent countless nights under the bright lights of strip clubs, dancing for strangers, seeking fleeting attention.

Her life was a web of destructive relationships, often with married men, including my husband. Families were torn apart. Trust was shattered. Hearts were broken. But she didn't care. She wore her choices like armor, parading around as though she were invincible, as though she were "all that and a bag of chips." She even bragged about destroying marriages, taking some sort of twisted pride in the chaos she caused. Who does that? Who finds joy in tearing others apart?

She had children from some of these relationships, but even they weren't spared from her recklessness. She passed them off to others as if they were burdens she couldn't be bothered to carry. Her actions caused pain, deep pain. Trauma rippled through the lives she touched, including mine.

She shattered my world. I had built a life with my husband—a life I believed in, a life I loved. But her presence destroyed our happiness. I won't pretend that I only blamed her. My ex-husband had his share of the blame, too. Still, it was her brazenness, her unapologetic cruelty, that made the betrayal cut so much deeper.

When I discovered the truth, it felt like a tidal wave of pain and devastation. More truth than my heart could bear. I wanted to beat her ass. I wanted her to feel the agony she had inflicted on me and countless others. And yet, when she saw that my marriage had crumbled, she vanished, moving on to her next victim, leaving wreckage in her wake without a second thought.

For years, I carried the weight of hate, anger, and despair. It wasn't just about losing my husband—it was about losing my sense of security, trust, and the life I had envisioned for myself. The trauma was overwhelming, pressing heavily on my heart, suffocating my spirit.

It was in one of my darkest nights that I found myself on my knees, crying out to God for strength. I was a Christian. I knew the importance of forgiveness, but how could I forgive someone who had caused so much intentional harm? How could I forgive someone who had brought so much pain into my life?

I won't lie—healing didn't come quickly or easily. It took over ten years before I could even whisper the words, "I forgive her," and even now, a part of me wonders if I have truly let go of all the anger. Some wounds take a lifetime to heal.

As I write these words, tears stream down my face. I pray to God to release any lingering pieces of resentment that still linger within me. I don't want to carry the burden of hate any longer. I want to be completely free—from the pain, from the anger, and from the harm she so intentionally caused to me and so many others.

Forgiveness is not about condoning her actions. It's about choosing to let go of the chains that keep me tied to the hurt. It's about finding peace within myself, even if she never seeks redemption. And so, I release it to God. I trust that He will heal the parts of me that still ache and fill the spaces that were left broken.

I choose freedom. I choose healing. I choose to live a life unburdened by her choices. And with God's help, I will continue to let go, one prayer at a time.

Matthew 6:14

"For if ye forgive men their trespasses, your heavenly Father will also forgive you: But if ye forgive not men their trespasses, neither will your Father forgive your trespasses"

King James Version (KJV)

Chapter #28

WHOSE AM I?
Natisha

For 16 years, I believed I knew exactly who I was. My identity was shaped by the individuals listed on my birth certificate and the family I grew up with—the family I thought was mine. But that all changed when I was 16.

One ordinary day, the girl I knew as a childhood friend showed up at my house with her dad for a hair appointment. My mother was her beautician, and this visit was part of their routine. But on this particular day, she revealed something that would shatter my understanding of myself: she was my sister. We shared the same father.

At first, I didn't believe her. How could I? But deep down, her words ignited something—a small voice that had always questioned my connection with the man I believed to be my father. I had brushed off those feelings, blaming them on my teenage moods or resentment over how he treated my mom. But now, the doubts seemed to carry weight.

As if to underscore the gravity of her revelation, she told me our grandmother had passed away. I cried, not because I knew this woman—how could I?—but because I felt I had been cheated. Cheated out of grandparents who attended school events, who created a sanctuary to visit, who left warm, lasting memories. Instead, I had fragmented recollections of my maternal grandparents and a paternal grandfather I barely knew. The grandmother I thought was mine had died in childbirth.

The weight of it all—her words, the truth—left me feeling cheated, hurt, confused, and angry. Yet, I stayed silent. The man I called "father" was still alive, and I couldn't bring myself to confront him with what I now suspected. I didn't even know if he was aware that I wasn't his biological child. So, we continued living the lie.

Fast forward to 2000. My "father" passed away from cancer. I was devastated. I sat by his bedside as he took his last breath, watching the monitor transition from numbers to question marks. Grief consumed me. And then, as if to twist the knife further, the man who was my biological father had the audacity to show up at the funeral. He claimed he was there to "pay his respects" and "check on me," but I knew the truth—he was there to see my mother.

Where was this concern for me all those years? Why now? The truth felt like a betrayal upon betrayal. My parents' marriage had never been perfect—I knew that. I even knew about the affairs. But to discover that I was the product of my mother's affair, her "dirty little secret"? That was a wound I didn't know how to heal.

Adding salt to the wound, I learned that select members of my maternal family had known all along. They had helped her keep this secret. When I confronted her, asking why she didn't just leave my "father" and take me with her if she was so unhappy, her response stunned me. She told me that my biological father was a drug addict with unsavory sexual proclivities.

But this was the man she chose. This was the man she loved for 12 years. And I was the product of that love.

The man I had called "father" was safe, stable, and a good provider. In contrast, my biological father was a heroin user, a cocaine snorter, and a womanizing sex addict. The shame I carried wasn't my own, but it felt like it was. I withdrew from my "father's" family, fearing they had always known and saw me as an outsider, a fraud.

When my mother passed away in 2005, grief pushed me to seek answers. There was no DNA test during her lifetime—just speculation. For my peace of mind, I finally sent away for a DNA kit and asked my biological father to participate. Reluctantly, he agreed.

When the results came in, I cried and prayed before opening the package. I wanted so desperately for the man who had raised me, who taught me to ride a bike, who cared for me when I was sick, to be my biological father. But as I read the results, my stomach sank. He wasn't.

I shared the news with my biological father. His response? "Are you happy now?" I told him the truth: "No." That was all it took for him to lash out in anger, cursing me over the phone. I hung up, feeling as though I'd experienced yet another death.

I'm the daughter of a former addict, a man who is selfish and emotionally incapable of genuine connection. How do I reconcile that? How do I forge a relationship, especially when he is someone I struggle to respect? I was angry—at him, at my dead mother, at the mess I had inherited. I didn't create it, but I was left to carry it.

It has taken, and continues to take, prayer, therapy, and self-reflection to release the shame and guilt that never belonged to me. I wrestle daily with my identity and the DNA that created me. I love my biological father for where he is today and for the 23 chromosomes he contributed—but that's it. I owe him nothing more. The father-daughter bond he wishes for isn't possible. I already had that bond with my dad, and he's gone.

The man who gave me life is my biological father. But the man who raised me, loved me, and stood by me—that man is my dad. He may not have been perfect, but he was present.

I would be lying if I said I was completely healed. I still cry over the circumstances of my birth. I still feel the sting of discovering another family I never knew existed. And yes, I still grapple with self-doubt in my marriage, friendships, and career. But in those moments, I remind myself—and the little girl still within me—that we are here for a reason.

God makes no mistakes. He can create miracles out of mayhem. I am dedicated to uncovering my purpose, to understanding why He chose to create me from this chaos. Through His love, the tools of therapy, self-reflection, and grace, I am learning to embrace myself fully.

I am not defined by the mess that created me. I am defined by the strength, faith, and resilience that keep me moving forward.

Psalms 147:3

"He healeth the broken in heart, and bindeth up their wounds."
King James Version (KJV)

Chapter #29

BUILT FROM BROKEN PIECES
Celestine

I went through life broken, carrying the weight of emotions that seemed too heavy to bear—abandonment, rejection, fear, anger, low self-esteem, insecurities, greed, impatience, and even hypertension. Born the youngest of four children in a single-parent household, I was surrounded by chaos from an early age. My siblings—two older sisters and a brother—rarely included me in their plans. My sisters didn't want me tagging along because they knew I'd tell on them for kissing boys or sneaking a smoke in the alley. My brother kept me away while he and his friends threw rocks at cars.

Alone, I would create worlds for myself. One moment, I'd be playing jacks, paddle ball, or with my baby dolls, and the next, I'd be chasing after friends, desperate to fit in. Yet, even surrounded by people, I felt down and lonely. I was constantly searching for something to make me feel good—something to fill the emptiness inside me.

My parents married at 15 and 16 but divorced by 20 with four children. My father struggled with addictions—to crack, gambling, and sex. My mother, left to raise us on her own, worked full-time and parented out of anger, fear, and resentment. While I always knew my mother loved me, I often felt like she didn't like me. She said and did hurtful things, but she also instilled in us discipline, prayer, and the importance of education. By God's grace, all of us graduated high school without children of our own, held jobs, and contributed to the household. For that, I admire her strength and resilience, though our relationship has always been rocky.

115

As I grew older, more broken pieces of me surfaced. I had an attitude problem, a sharp tongue, and a competitive streak that left no room for grace. I was greedy, envious, and mean-spirited, often complaining and never satisfied. My insecurities grew into a desperate need for attention, acceptance, and validation. I became promiscuous, searching for love and security in all the wrong places. I felt like a mistake, a constant mess-up, unworthy of love.

I got my first job at 15, graduated high school at 18, and just a few months later, my mom put me out. My struggles with drinking, weed smoking, and promiscuity were still spiraling out of control. At 18, I started seeing a 28-year-old man. By 23, I became pregnant and had my first child. At 26, I was snorting cocaine. By 27, I was smoking weed joints laced with crack, and before the year ended, I was smoking crack outright.

Acts 27:44 (NKJV):

"And the rest, some on boards, and some on broken pieces of the ship. And so it came to pass, that they escaped all safely to land."

I feel like my life is a puzzle with many broken pieces, but God has been building me, piece by piece, from those shattered fragments. Without knowing I had the disease of addiction—a generational curse heavy in my father's bloodline, as well as among many of my aunts, uncles, and cousins—I overlooked my struggles as mere bad habits. After the birth of my first child, my life began to take a darker turn. My drinking, marijuana use, and nonstop partying seemed normal to me. I would brush it off, thinking, *"This is just what grown folks do. We turn up."* But deep down, I was in denial about my issues. One year later, I lost my house, my car, and my job, all to my uncontrollable drug habits. Shame, guilt, denial, anger, and fear consumed me, and the drugs only amplified those emotions to unbearable heights.

I am the mother of two daughters, ages nine and one. Both have the same father, a man 10 years older than me. Looking back, I realize I sought relationships with older men because I was searching for security, validation, love, and, most of all, a father figure. At 15, I began working my first job. By 16, I bought my first car. By 18, I was out of my mother's house, desperate to grow up. I thought I knew what I wanted in a man. My daughters' father had been at his job for 10 years, had his own place, and drove a car. I thought, *"This man's got it together."* It didn't bother me that he already had four kids and two baby mamas. In fact, his commitment to paying child support for all his children told me he was responsible, unlike my own absent father. I ignored the red flags, even when I caught him still sleeping with one of his baby mamas.

My drug use spiraled out of control. A few days after a family reunion, my aunt called an intervention with my mom, my oldest sister, and me. She told me she had contacted women's recovery houses in Fort Wayne, IN, looking for a bed for me. They didn't sugarcoat their concerns about my life. They asked, *"Do you want to go?"* I hesitated, saying in a low, shaky voice, *"But I don't want to leave my kids."* That's when I heard the Holy Spirit whisper, *"You already left them."* That truth hit me hard. My daughters were living with their father, visiting me sporadically because I was unstable. I was there in body sometimes, but not emotionally or financially. I had abandoned them in every way that mattered. So, I agreed to go. That weekend, their father and my two girls drove me to a halfway house in Fort Wayne.

At the halfway house, I was introduced to Narcotics Anonymous (N/A). I managed to stay clean for 14 months, started attending church with one of the staff members, and was making progress. But I relapsed, falling back into my addiction for five months before searching for another recovery home. I was accepted into the Genesis House, a faith-based recovery program. This time, I fully surrendered to God to the best of my ability. I applied myself more seriously to recovery, my relationship with God, and my spiritual growth. I got baptized again, was filled with the Holy Spirit, speaking in tongues, and started serving in the church. I led the transportation ministry, became the head usher, and eventually became an ordained minister. I also became an early childhood teacher, learning better parenting skills and healthier ways to communicate and discipline.

In 2009, the Lord delivered me from cigarettes. In 2010, I became pregnant again, and in 2011, I gave birth to another beautiful daughter. My journey with God deepened as I learned what it meant to be a leader in the body of Christ. One evening, I felt led to study 2 Chronicles 7:14: *"If my people, who are called by my name, will humble themselves and pray and seek my face and turn from their wicked ways, then I will hear from heaven, and I will forgive their sin and will heal their land."* As I meditated on this verse, I felt a deep conviction and a renewed sense of purpose.

God's work in my life wasn't easy. The flesh still tempted me, and there were challenges. I bought a house through Habitat for Humanity, and my oldest daughter came to live with me. While I was proud of my progress, I still longed for a husband. My patterns of dating older men with jobs, homes, and cars persisted, but they often left me feeling rejected and unworthy. That rejection fueled anger and resentment, emotions I now recognize as lies from the enemy.

In 2015, I became a homeowner, held a full-time job, and managed life as a single mom. But the weight of doing it all alone became overwhelming. I stopped attending recovery meetings, and complacency set in. I began dating a man from church, but our relationship was plagued with insecurity and disorder. We fell into fornication, which weakened my spirit. When he ended things, I was devastated, angry, and filled with shame. This relapse spiraled into a seven-year battle with addiction.

Eventually, I cried out to God, asking for help. He delivered me in a way I didn't expect—through an arrest. That arrest marked the turning point in my life. I reconnected with a man named Doug, someone I had met years earlier through a recovery ministry at church. Doug, who was still clean and walking with the Lord, became a steady presence in my life. God spoke clearly to me, saying, *"I'm not giving you what you want; I'm giving you what you need."* Doug and I began dating, and our relationship blossomed. We got married on October 8, 2023, and have been growing together in faith ever since.

Those broken pieces God has rebuilt me from are many:

- **Rejection to Accepted**
- **Abandoned to Reclaimed**
- **Lost to Found**
- **Beatdown to Built Up**
- **Ugly Duckling to Beautiful Swan**

The Lord has truly given me beauty for ashes. While I still struggle with insecurities, I know that His work in me is ongoing. I've learned that my story isn't just about me—it's about God, His glory, and the souls He wants to reach through my testimony. With every step forward, I am reminded of His grace, and I stand as a living testament to His transformative power.

Hebrews 4:16

"Let us therefore come boldly unto the throne of grace, that we may
obtain mercy, and find grace to help in time of need."
King James Version (KJV)

Chapter #30

<u>LOVE, LOSS & RESILIENCE</u>
Nita

My childhood best friend, Marisa, introduced us in college. We were two 19-year-olds with birthdays just 21 days apart. From the moment we met, Brian and I shared a passionate, youthful kind of love—the kind that makes you feel invincible. But our fairy tale took a dark turn when Brian fell into the clutches of drug addiction. It tore us apart.

Brian knew I was a Christian girl, someone who wouldn't tolerate the path he was heading down. So, he ended the relationship, leaving me heartbroken and devastated. Our lives took separate paths. Over the years, we each found love elsewhere, married, and started families.

Brian's marriage was tumultuous, plagued by the demons of his addiction, and it ended after five years. My marriage was rooted in faith and God, yet we were unequally yoked. I was married to a kind man, an amazing father to our daughter, but our union lacked the connection and fulfillment I longed for. After 26 years of marriage, many tears, and countless prayers, I made the heart-wrenching decision to file for divorce.

Fate, however, had a different plan for Brian and me. Almost 30 years after our paths had diverged, they crossed again. By then, Brian had been drug-free for 14 years and had grown closer to God. The deep connection we once shared reignited as if no time had passed.

We decided to give love another chance. For a year and a half, we rebuilt what we thought was lost, blending our lives and families with hope and faith at the center. Eventually, we married, embarking on a new chapter together.

But life had challenges in store for us. When we reconnected, I knew Brian had congestive heart failure and kidney failure. I believed we had time before his health would decline. Yet, just a year into our marriage, those conditions took a toll, testing the very foundations of our love and commitment.

The day Brian gasped for breath and slipped into the grips of death remains etched in my memory as a nightmare I'll never forget. Watching helplessly as he fought for his life, I anointed his head with oil and prayed fervently for a miracle.

For nine minutes and twenty-seven seconds, paramedics worked to revive him. When they did, it felt like a small victory in a much larger battle. He remained in a coma for four days, and the doctors prepared me for the worst. They warned that if Brian survived, he might have significant brain damage and be unable to function as the man I once knew.

But Brian emerged, defying the odds. While his survival was a miracle, it marked the beginning of a new, more arduous chapter. He faced depression and the grueling toll of kidney dialysis three times a week. His body was weakened, his spirit burdened.

As a Christian, I turned to God for the strength to endure. I sought spiritual and professional support, recognizing the importance of caring for myself so I could continue caring for Brian. My journey became one of healing and self-discovery, learning to balance my role as his caregiver with my own emotional and mental health.

During this time, our family was hit with wave after wave of loss. We mourned Brian's brother, father, and grandmother, as well as my two aunts and brother-in-law. These moments tested us, but they also strengthened our faith.

When we recently learned that Brian's calcification in his arteries had increased and he no longer qualified for a kidney transplant, my heart sank. But my faith did not waver. In the midst of it all, I still trust God.

Brian and I face each day with courage, resilience, and an unwavering belief in God's plan. Our love has become a beacon of light amidst life's storms, a reminder that even in the darkest moments, there is hope.

Ours is a story of love, loss, and resilience. It is a testament to the enduring power of faith and the strength of the human spirit. Together, we have weathered unimaginable challenges, bound by a love that has withstood the test of time.

Through every trial, we hold tightly to the belief that with God, all things are possible. It is not easy, but it is possible. And in that truth, we find the courage to keep going, to keep loving, and to keep trusting in the One who holds us both in His hands.

Matthew 19:26

"But Jesus beheld them, and said unto them, With men this is impossible; but with God all things are possible."
King James Version (KJV)

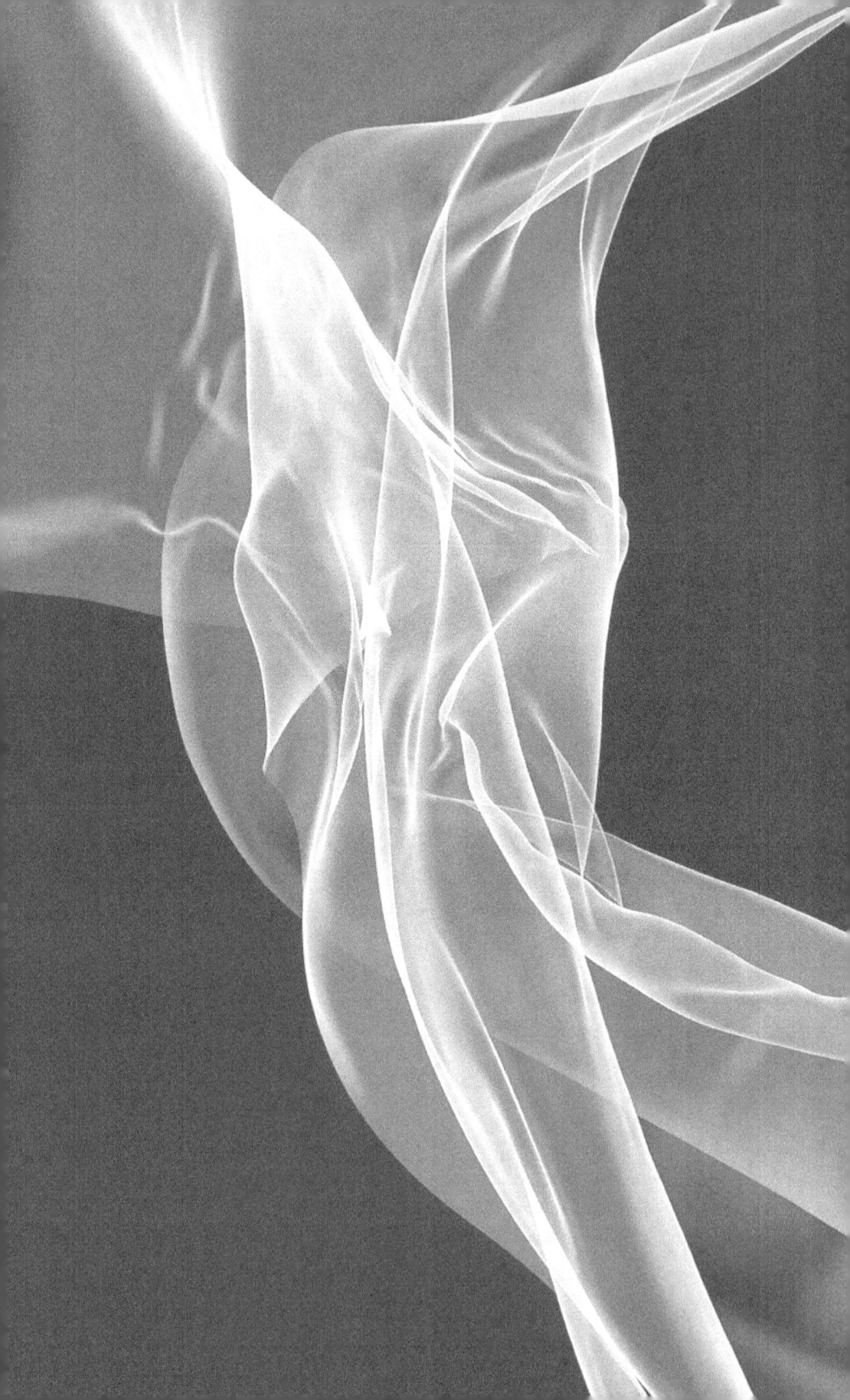

Chapter #31

<u>NOT THE FIRST PICK</u>
Treva Datcher

She didn't choose me first.
She didn't end up choosing me at all.
If I knew who he was, I'd ask him if he would've chosen me.
Eventually, I was chosen, but the anger of not being chosen superseded any positive emotions I might have felt.

As life went on, more people began to choose me, but their "yes" didn't erase the sting of the "no's."
Mistaken for a manager or team mom far too many times, I learned to always keep my resume in my pocket.

But one day, God revealed through His Word that I was His first pick all along.
Someone had been thinking of me all along!
Who knew that someone else's problem would become my purpose?

Adoption is a bittersweet process. You hear things like, *"Happy Gotcha Day,"* a phrase meant to be celebratory. But even in its joy, it carries an undertone—a reminder that the child was being rescued from something.

To this day, I have yet to confirm the identity of my father. And believe me, God willing, that conversation will happen someday. But adoption, when not properly processed, can plant deep roots of anger, abandonment, rejection, and those infamous "mommy and daddy" issues.

For me, it was incredibly hard to receive love in any form because love wasn't first nature for me. As I grew into adulthood, I went through a long season where I had no desire to be married or to have a family. I didn't feel I'd be of any value to anyone. After all, how could I offer love to someone else when I didn't fully understand what it meant to receive it?

Eventually, I began to see God's favor manifest through athletics. I was hired to coach high school golf—both boys and girls. Yet, even in this role, I faced the same recurring doubts.

"Are you helping out?"
"Is your daughter on the team?"

These questions came at me multiple times a week, causing me to question myself and my validity. Each time, I explained, *"No, I'm the coach,"* and what followed was either an awkward apology or another layer of questioning: "What's your college career like? What are your stats? How many years of experience do you have?"

The constant need to prove my place as a young woman of color in this field wore on me. I often wondered how much time I spent defending my position instead of pouring fully into the girls I was coaching.

Eventually, I humbled myself and fell on my face in prayer. I asked God to change my heart about being adopted. He led me to Psalm 139:13-16, and for the first time, I saw the truth clearly: God had been thinking about me long before my biological mother or father had the chance to not choose me.

This revelation changed everything. I began to understand that I wasn't an afterthought; I was intentionally crafted. God needed me, and I needed to reach this very point in my life to fully grasp that truth.

With a changed perspective and an open heart, I found myself propelled toward the purpose God had for me. One of the most profound moments came when I had the chance to counsel one of my players through her own adoption journey.

Because of my past—every trial, every tear—I knew exactly what to say to her. I was able to offer guidance, comfort, and hope in a way that only someone who had walked a similar path could.

The road to this understanding wasn't easy, but I wouldn't trade it for anything. If I had to go through it all over again, I would—but this time, with the wisdom and perspective I have now.

God showed me that my identity isn't tied to who didn't choose me, but to the One who always has. I am His first pick. And in Him, I've found purpose, healing, and the ability to help others navigate their own journeys.

I've learned that God's plans are always intentional, even when they start with broken pieces. And now, I stand here whole, ready to share His love and fulfill the purpose He always had in mind for me.

Psalms 139:13-16

"For thou hast possessed my reins: thou hast covered me in my mother's womb. I will praise thee; for I am fearfully *and* wonderfully made: marvelous *are* thy works; and *that* my soul knoweth right well. My substance was not hid from thee, when I was made in secret, *and* curiously wrought in the lowest parts of the earth. Thine eyes did see my substance, yet being unperfect; and in thy book all *my members* were written, *which* in continuance were fashioned, when *as yet there was* none of them."

King James Version (KJV)

Chapter #32

<u>HIS VOICE MAKES A DIFFERENCE</u>
Lorna

I had a very humble beginning and lived a sheltered life in a Christian family. I never experienced the things many teenagers were exposed to and, looking back, I realize I was very naive about life's challenges.

When I was in my first year of high school, my father passed away. It was a loss that left a void in my heart, and I yearned for a father figure. I never dated during my school years; instead, I remained focused on my goals, determined to help my mother as she struggled to raise four fatherless children.

At 17, I was baptized and began my walk with the Lord. By age 19, I met and fell in love with a man. We dated for two years, and I held on to my Christian values and beliefs. At 21, we got married, and I entered what I thought would be a happy and loving union.

But within three months of marriage, my perspective on love and marriage began to unravel. My husband, ten years my senior, showed me a side of marriage I had never seen between my mother and father. I was disrespected, unloved, and unsupported, despite my efforts to show love and do my best as a wife. I didn't understand what was happening, and because I never learned to communicate my feelings, I bottled everything inside. I couldn't share my pain—not with my mother, my siblings, or anyone.

It was then I realized my husband was promiscuous. By 22, we had our first child, and by 24, we welcomed our second. I had a full-time job and was managing the home with little or no support from him. I had no choice but to hire a live-in helper to care for the children. The arguments became constant. I felt more alone than ever. I wore a constant smile, but behind it, no one could imagine the pain I carried.

Four years into the marriage, the truth hit me like a tidal wave. My husband had lied to me. When we met, he claimed to have one child, but I discovered he had six other children—six! The betrayal and stress were unbearable. I decided I didn't want those children coming to our home. The only one I welcomed was the child I had known about before our marriage. This, of course, became another source of conflict.

The worst part was his blatant disrespect. He would bring women into our home whenever I wasn't there. When I questioned him, the confrontation turned loud and aggressive. My home, which should have been a place of peace, became a living nightmare. The verbal abuse soon turned physical.

I'll never forget one evening, during a simple game of checkers. He was winning every round and teasing me, but when I finally won a game and joked back, his mood shifted. In a fit of anger, he threw his boot at me, hitting my left ear. I fell to the floor, spitting blood. My eardrum was fractured. I was in pain—physically, emotionally, and spiritually. I started praying to God, *"Lord, deliver me from this violent man."*

It didn't stop there. I soon discovered my helper was pregnant with his child. Before I could fully process this betrayal, I learned he had another baby with a girl from our community. I was overwhelmed. I didn't have the skills, experience, or support to handle it all. My world was collapsing around me.

One evening, the burden became too much. An argument pushed me to the edge, and I decided to end my life. My husband was sitting at the dining table when I walked into the kitchen, sharpened a knife, and told him, *"I can't do this anymore. I'm going to end it all."* Without hesitation, he grabbed the car keys and said, *"I'm leaving. I don't want the police questioning me."* He left the house, leaving me broken and alone.

Two babies slept peacefully in the house as I walked to the back, climbed a naseberry tree, and raised the knife to my neck. My mind was made up. But in that moment, a voice—a loud, clear voice—pierced through my despair and froze me in place.

"REMEMBER JOB."

Those words stunned me. My hand dropped, the knife fell, and I still don't know how I got down from that tree. It was as if God Himself had reached into the darkness and pulled me back.

My husband returned just before dawn, likely expecting to find a tragedy. Instead, I was inside, praising the Lord for His deliverance. The look of disappointment on his face said it all, but I didn't care. God had saved me.

I share this story because I know someone out there may be going through something similar. You might feel alone, hopeless, or broken, but let me tell you this: **God is able.**

No matter what you're facing, no matter how deep the pain, hold on to His promises. God never goes back on His word. He said in Jeremiah 29:11, *"For I know the plans I have for you,"* declares the *LORD, "plans to prosper you and not to harm you, plans to give you hope and a future."*

Our God is truly AWESOME. Today, I am walking in my divine purpose. I am healed, whole, and a living testament to God's faithfulness. If you haven't accepted Him into your life yet, I urge you—don't wait. Tomorrow is not promised. Allow God to be your anchor and your deliverer.

He has done it for me, and I know He will do it for you. God bless.

Jeremiah 29:11

"For I know the thoughts that I think toward you, saith the LORD, thoughts of peace, and not of evil, to give you an expected end."
King James Version (KJV)

Chapter #33

YEA, THOUGH I WALK THE VALLEY OF THE SHADOW OF DEATH

Carol Gray-Greenway

When I heard my doctor say, *"You have stage III blood cancer,"* I knew my life was about to change—physically, financially, mentally, and spiritually.

Physically, the toll was overwhelming: weight loss, nausea, vomiting, hair loss, bone pain, no appetite, neuropathy, and relentless fatigue, to name a few. I endured a year of chemotherapy treatments, blood draws, scans, biopsies, and countless other interventions to fight this disease.

There were days when I wasn't sure what God's plan was, but I pushed through, knowing that with God, my faithful and loving husband Mike, and the prayers of family, friends, and even strangers, I could face each day. Did I mention how incredible Mike has been through it all? He came to every appointment, wiped my tears after biopsies, stayed with me in the hospital every day for two weeks, and placed cool cloths on my neck while I vomited endlessly. Having someone here on earth to walk with you in the hardest moments is a blessing beyond words.

Before every appointment, I would pause at the hospital doors and whisper, *"You first, Jesus."*

The financial challenges were daunting. Before my illness, Mike and I were both working and living comfortably. But cancer came with astronomical costs—medications alone could be $14,000 for a 21-

day supply. Despite having insurance, the extra costs added up quickly. Yet, through it all, we never missed a bill payment. We continued to live comfortably. *That's God!*

Your Faith can move mountains, and your doubt can create them! Never doubt God! You have two choices when you are in a situation. You can sit in your self-pity and give up or you can fight! Some may say "but the anxiety is overwhelming." I say our anxiety does not come from thinking about the future, but from wanting to control it! Give God complete control!

Mentally, the battle was fierce. There were moments when my mind whispered, *"You can't withstand the storm,"* and I had to reply, *"I am the storm!"*

I drew strength from my faith, which had been instilled in me as a child. *"Train up a child in the way that they should go, and they will not depart from it!"*

At the time of my diagnosis, my life was already filled with challenges. I had moved across the country to support my husband's military career, leaving family and friends behind. My mother was battling end-stage dementia, and my father, at 91, was facing his own health struggles. I felt drained, unable to be there for my parents, but God wrapped my mind in peace, reminding me that He is in control.

My mama always said, *"You gotta always trust and believe in Jesus!"* Even in her last days, when I whispered His name, her eyes lit up, and a faint smile graced her lips. Her unwavering faith continues to inspire me.

My Spiritual Change Was Amazing!

The morning I was admitted into the hospital for my stem cell transplant, I was given a large dose of chemotherapy (melphalan), a treatment so powerful it kills everything except your organs. In that moment, I felt a deep cleansing, as though something within me was being renewed. The next day, I received my stem cells, and it was as if life was being restored inside me.

As everything began working together for good, I developed a fever. I was iced down from my head to my feet, and I was told I would get much worse before I would feel better. That night, as I lay there weak and exhausted, I told my husband to go home and get some rest. It was just me and God in that hospital room, and I felt as though I was walking through *the valley of the shadow of death.*

You see, you must pray the hardest when it's hardest to pray. I was very sick, but I began to pray for healing. I asked God to give me a sign that everything was going to be alright. I thanked Him—oh, how I thanked Him! I thanked Him for my children, my grandchildren, their spouses and significant others, and my extended family. I thanked Him for His grace and mercy, for bringing me this far on my journey. As I closed my eyes, a single tear rolled down my cheek and fell onto my pillow.

Suddenly, the machines I was hooked up to began to flash and beep with alarms. I opened my eyes, startled, and the nurse ran into the room. *"Are you okay?"* she asked with concern. I smiled and said, *"Oh yes! God just let me know everything will be alright."*

The machines went back to normal, but since she was already in the room, she decided to draw my blood from my port. She struggled to get the blood flowing, and then I slowly raised my hand to the heavens and said, *"Jesus, open it."* At that very moment, the blood began to flow into the tube. The nurse looked at me, astonished, and said, *"What just happened?"* I smiled again and answered, *"Jesus just happened."*

Shaking her head, she laughed softly and said, *"You are full of surprises tonight!"* Without missing a beat, I responded, *"No, I'm full of Jesus."* She checked my temperature, and to her amazement, it was going down. God was moving in a mighty way! There was no denying His presence in that room.

That night, I came to a beautiful realization: I know God can heal my body, and if He does, that's a win. But if He doesn't, it's still a win because I will be one step closer to seeing His face and living in eternal happiness. As Christians, our ultimate goal is to hear those precious words, *"Well done, my good and faithful servant."*

So, I urge you to love one another as Jesus loves us. Forgive often, as Jesus has forgiven you. Let His light shine through you so that others may find their way to the King. Read the Bible daily because a dusty Bible prepares for a dirty life. Pray daily. Love everyone. And if you ever find yourself walking through *the valley of the shadow of death,* remember this: *"Fear no evil, for thou art with you."*

May His rod and His staff comfort you.

Psalms 23:4

"Yea, though I walk through the valley of the shadow of death,
I will fear no evil: for thou art with me; thy rod and thy staff
they comfort me."
King James Version (KJV)

Chapter #34

<u>GOD WILL PROVIDE</u>
Bridget

I was born with meningitis. The doctors told my mom I might not make it through the night, and if I did, she would have to care for me for the rest of my life. You're probably wondering, *What is meningitis?* Meningitis is an inflammation of the brain and spinal cord membranes, typically caused by an infection. It can be viral, bacterial, or fungal, and symptoms include headache, fever, and stiff neck. While some cases resolve on their own, others can be life-threatening, requiring immediate antibiotic treatment.

My aunt stepped in to help prepare my mom for the journey ahead, providing her with numerous medical books about meningitis. My mom, a new single mother with a sick baby, had no idea of the road God was preparing her to travel. But she placed her faith in Him, and He gave her the strength and knowledge to care for me.

Throughout school, I struggled—homework, book reports, quizzes, and tests all felt like mountains I couldn't climb. I remember receiving assignments back with a big red "F" marked at the top, while my classmates had passing grades. My mom did everything she could to support me. She paid for tutors, took me to be tested, and finally, a doctor diagnosed me with short-term memory loss.

People don't realize how hard it was for me to take the same tests repeatedly, only to fail again. I cried more times than I could count, desperate to just pass like the other students.

One time, a teacher gave me the test and the answers the day before. All I had to do was study and take the same test the next day. I studied hard, determined to succeed. But when the time came, I failed again—even with the answers in front of me the day before. I simply could not retain the information.

Despite the struggles, I can confidently say that God has never left me nor forsaken me. Hebrews 13:5 says, *"Never will I leave you; never will I forsake you."* Since October 18, 1977—the day I was born—God has been by my side.

I've endured trauma in my life, but through it all, God has always seen me as His creation. And let me tell you something: God doesn't make mistakes.

My grandma Mary always called me "special." For a long time, I didn't like that word because of the way my classmates used it to tease me. They called me "special" as an insult, and it hurt deeply.

But my grandma? She used the word differently. She called me "special" because she saw the potential God had placed in me. She recognized the gifts and talents He had given me long before the foundation of the world. My mom saw it too.

Though I've faced trauma—and still endure some of it today—I know that God has always been there. My mom has never left my side, and I thank God for her presence in my life. Trauma may have tried to break me, but *Jehovah Jireh*—God, my Provider—has been my refuge.

God never promised my life would be perfect, but He has walked with me every step of the way. Through the pain, the struggles, and the tears, He has remained faithful.

I've learned that while trauma may leave its mark, God's grace is bigger. He has conquered every burden at the cross. My life is far from perfect, but I can stand tall knowing this truth: *I have trauma, but I also have God in my life.*

Hebrews 13:5

"Let your conversation be without covetousness; and be content with such things as ye have: for he hath said, I will never leave thee, nor forsake thee."
King James Version (KJV)

Chapter #35

IN THE QUIET OF VOWS
Nita

In the quiet of vows, where love shining bright,
Two hearts united, a promise alight.
Hand in hand, they danced through life's gentle sway,
But shadows of anger crept into their day.

With every whispered word, joy painted their dreams,
Yet beneath soft laughter, a tempest would gleam.
From calm to chaos, like lightning his words would ignite,
Screams pierced the silence, echoes of battles out of sight.

In the grip of his emotions, her heart turned to stone,
For the man she adored was a stranger, internally alone.
With curses like dagger, moments fractured the light,
Yet she called upon God for she knew of His might.

Yet love, deep and steadfast, held firm in her chest,
Though the hands that once cherished now left her distressed.
She would not be silenced, nor caged in despair,
For love's truest essence is knowing what's fair.

They prayed to the heavens, sought healing divine,
With faith as their anchor, they would weather the brine.
In the warmth of forgiveness, they nurtured their wounds,
Finding strength in the struggle, where compassion blooms.

Together they ventured through valleys of pain,
Unraveling traumas, the hurt and the stain.
With each session of therapy, a step forward to the light,
He learned to confront what had haunted his night.

Through God's gentle whispers, the darkness grew small,
As love became armor, they began to stand tall.
Hand in hand, they journeyed, through the storms of strife,
Two souls intertwined, reclaiming their life.

Now laughter rings freely, where shadows once lay,
With grace in their hearts, they have found their own way.
Though trials may linger, and storms may still brew,
With the help of God, she has found strength anew.

Isaiah 12:2

"Behold, God *is* my salvation; I will trust, and not be afraid: for the LORD JEHOVAH *is* my strength and *my* song; he also is become my salvation."

King James Version (KJV)

Chapter #36

LIKE ST. STEPHEN
Julie

Ugly.
Fat.
Stupid.
Retarded.
Obnoxious.

These were the stones you hurled at me, again and again, during my delicate girlhood.

Each sharp edge made its impression, piercing my soul and shaping who I was becoming.

Like St. Stephen, I accepted them without complaint, hands outstretched, bracing for more.

Like St. Stephen, you named me: *Julia Stephens*, a youthful martyr to your anger.

In whispered conversations, you wondered why I wasn't like the other girls.

Ugly. Fat. Stupid. Retarded. Obnoxious. *How could I be?*

Yet, like St. Stephen, the light of God pierced through each gash, transforming the wounds into radiance.

Like St. Stephen, His love prevailed, and I became.

Beautiful. Perfect. Smart. Determined. Joyful.

Proverbs 9:6

"Forsake the foolish, and live; and go in the way of understanding."
King James Version (KJV)

Chapter #37

FORCED TO GROW UP TOO QUICKLY
Anonymous

"You know that it's OK not to get married. Boys don't like fat girls." My mother said this to me when I was 16. I remember it so vividly. I was standing in the kitchen after school and track practice, stunned. There was no rhyme or reason for her to say something so hurtful, but she said it anyway. I had always sensed something was different between us, but those words made me question everything— Did she love me? Did she even like me? Or was her love for me simply an obligation because I was her daughter?

My childhood was defined by 364 days—the number of days between my sister's birth and mine. I was the firstborn, and from the moment my mother knew she was pregnant again, my life was accelerated. I had to walk before my sister was born. I had to be potty trained before she arrived. I even learned to pull on door handles to signal I needed help with the bathroom. My mother was so worried about having two babies close in age that I was forced to grow up before I was ready. I met milestones early, but at the cost of my childhood.

This forced independence shaped me. I became an eternal people-pleaser, always striving to make sure everyone was okay, always seeking approval. To this day, I catch myself saying, "I'm sorry. Are you mad at me?"—a direct result of how I was raised.

There was never a birthday that was just mine. We always celebrated on the same day. I was different, the "bigger" one. I was always tall and sturdy, off the charts as a baby. When I was three, I looked like I should be five; when I was five, I looked like I should be eight. My sister, in contrast, was average—just a normal-sized child—which made things harder. She was coddled, while I was expected to hold my own.

As a child, my father was my saving grace. We were kindred spirits—walking the same, talking the same, even sharing mannerisms. We were both serious and driven. Sports and the fine arts connected us: he played the viola; I played the violin. He was a basketball and track athlete; I thrived in water polo, swimming, and track and field—specifically shot put and discus. My bond with my father carried me through my childhood and teenage years. As I grew older, our connection only deepened. My mother noticed this and resented it. I'll never forget her saying in my 30s, "Oh, I know your father was your savior."

That bond with my father contrasted sharply with my strained relationship with my mother. She connected immediately with my sister, and that divide was clear in both her words and actions. When I would try to hug her, she'd push me away and say, "Get off me." Meanwhile, my sister would sit next to her on the couch as my mother scratched her ear to soothe her. I didn't realize the depth of this rejection until I reflected on it as an adult.

Now, as I navigate my medical challenges, I understand that my mother never wanted to understand me. She still doesn't. I have learned to protect myself. I choose when to call her, when to pick up the phone. The irony of her words, *"Friendship is a two-way street,"* doesn't escape me. She doesn't reciprocate, and that message is loud and clear.

Leaving for college was liberating. It marked the beginning of my journey to self-acceptance. For the first time, I was free to define myself. I was no longer under her control or criticism. College gave me independence—a gateway to healing. Yet, coming home during the summers was a stark contrast. At school, I could be my own person, but at home, I was back under her rules. Let's face it: it was *her* rules. She controlled the family, and everyone knew it.

Graduating college was another defining point. I earned my degree, was dating a loving, Christian man, and was ready to start a new chapter in a small town. Even though I had accomplished great things, my mother always seemed to get the best of me. I was 22 years old; how could things still bother me? But they did. My mother's words always lingered. Before I started my first job, she took me shopping and said, *"You know a size 24 is the largest they carry in department stores. Once you go beyond that, you can't shop here anymore."* I tried to let those words go, but they stayed with me, echoing in my mind for years. What stung most was the hypocrisy: she stood at 350 pounds when she said it then, and now she is a lean 150 pounds.

At 24, the man I'd been dating proposed, and I was beyond excited. He accepted me, and I felt safe with him. Our wedding was beautiful. My orchestra conductor and his string quartet played, and our closest friends sang for the unity candle lighting. Yet even on my wedding day, my mother found a way to belittle me in front of others. Seeing me in wrinkled clothes after getting my hair and makeup done with my bridesmaids, she looked at me and said, *"You wore that to the salon?"* It was a power play, another attempt to make me feel insignificant.

The first few years of marriage were hard. My husband and I were learning to live together and adjust to each other's habits. One day, he looked at me and gently said, *"You're showing some of the same characteristics your mom does with depression and anxiety. I think it might help if you talked to someone."* At first, I was in denial. *No, that couldn't be me. That wasn't me.* But as time went on and I continued to feel weighed down by so many unspoken emotions, I realized he was right. I needed help—help from someone outside of my marriage.

That moment marked the beginning of a journey that changed my life for the better.

Through a combination of medication, cognitive behavioral therapy, and EMDR (eye movement desensitization and reprocessing) therapy, I came to understand the truth about my trauma. It wasn't physical trauma, but emotional trauma—mental wounds that had left scars I didn't realize were there. As a child, I believed trauma only came in certain forms. I told myself, *"You can't have trauma. You grew up in a two-parent home. Both your parents worked. They provided for you, even paid for college. You had a good life."* But I was wrong.

Deep down, I always felt my mother treated me differently, but I never had confirmation. Any time I confronted her about it, she denied it. *"I love you and your sister the same,"* she'd insist. I knew it wasn't true, but I had no proof—no validation—until a trip I took with my two aunts, whom I'm incredibly close to. I was 30 years old and finally brave enough to ask them the hard questions:

"Was I treated differently? Did my mother reject me? Did she not understand me—or worse, did she understand me and choose not to?"

Their answers were both painful and liberating. They confirmed what I had always suspected. My mother didn't understand me, and she didn't want to. My grandmother had seen it too. My aunts shared how odd it was, given that my mother herself had experienced a lack of understanding from *her* mother. Why would she pass that same hurt onto me? My aunts also revealed that my similarities to my father were a source of tension. My mother felt threatened because being like him made me harder for her to connect with.

That conversation was a turning point in my mental health journey. I wasn't crazy. I wasn't imagining things. The emotional trauma I carried from my childhood was real, and it had followed me into adulthood.

Fast forward 20 years, and I can now say I am in the best mental and emotional shape of my life. I have a job I love, and I fully accept myself for who I am. Yes, I'm emotional. Yes, I'm sensitive. Yes, I wear my heart on my sleeve. But I've come to understand that these qualities aren't flaws—they're part of what makes me *me*. They're what make me human. I love who I am. I love who I've become.

I cherish the close relationship I have with my father, and I no longer care that it bothers my mother. I don't seek her approval anymore because I don't need it. Her opinions, her reactions—they don't hold power over me. It's taken years to get to this point, but I've learned that the only approval I need is God's.

Through Him, I have found my strength. He has laid the path before me, opening doors and presenting opportunities for growth and healing. He is the reason I wake up every morning with purpose. He is the reason I stand tall today.

Life will always have its ups and downs, but I've learned to keep my eyes on the Lord. Without Him, I would have nothing. He has been my protector, my guide, and my constant companion. No matter what comes my way, I know God will continue to love me, strengthen me, and lead me forward. For that, I am forever grateful.

1 John 4:16

"And we have known and believed the love that God hath to us.
God is love; and he that dwelleth in love dwelleth in God,
and God in him."
King James Version (KJV)

Chapter #38

COMING OUT of MY EGYPT
Wendy Hazel

"I never thought I would make it out. Looking back, it felt like every part of my life was designed to break me. But what I couldn't see then was that God was setting the stage all along. Each battle, each trauma, was part of His plan, preparing me for something greater. I wasn't being destroyed—I was being refined for my divine purpose."

I was fifteen when my world collapsed. I still remember her last words as I stood right next to her: "Lord, what is this on me?" She started falling, and I tried to catch her so she wouldn't hit the ground too hard. I remember riding in the ambulance, her still unconscious, and waiting at the emergency room. The next day, my aunt took me to visit her, but just like that, she was gone. One moment, she was fine; the next, she was gone, leaving a gaping hole in my life.

At fifteen, you're barely a person. I was just beginning to figure out who I was, and now, I had to do it without her. My mother was my anchor, and now I was adrift. Nothing made sense. I would lie on my bed, remembering her voice, but she never came in to wake me up again. Suddenly, I was forced to grow up. There wasn't room to fall apart because life doesn't pause when your world does. Grief makes you vulnerable, and at the time, I didn't even realize how much I was drowning in it.

I met him two years later. He was everything I thought I needed: older, charming, and comforting. He filled the void left by my mother's absence—or so I thought. But looking back, I now realize he was preying on my vulnerability, manipulating the cracks in my spirit.

The relationship started like many abusive ones do—beautiful, with promise—until the real darkness came. The first time he hit me, I froze. I couldn't process it. I remember staring at my reflection afterward, wondering how I had become this woman—a woman with bruises. But I stayed. Like so many women, I thought I could fix it. I thought I could fix him.

Over time, the abuse escalated. He controlled so many aspects of my life—who I spoke to, where I went. I became a shell of the person I had been. I knew God all along—my mom had taught me the 23rd Psalm and the Lord's Prayer. I had faith in a God who was always a prayer away. One night in London, I surrendered completely. I prayed, "Lord, change my life. I can't live this way anymore."

He heard me and answered my prayer.

Fourteen years into that relationship, it almost killed me. One night, he left me bleeding. A stab wound so close to my heart, I thought it was the end.

But it wasn't.

God had other plans. I survived, but the emotional scars lingered long after. Even though I walked away, the trauma of that relationship stayed with me. Healing my body was one thing, but healing my soul was another.

I learned to forgive—not for him, but for me.

Years later, I faced the unthinkable: the sudden, tragic death of my only child. Nothing prepares you for losing a child. Nothing. That kind of pain—it's indescribable. It consumes you. I would sit alone in the middle of the night, feeling physical pain in my chest, as though a hook was pulling my heart out of my body.

Why, God? Why would You let this happen after everything I'd already endured? My son's death felt like the final blow. But even through my questions, I never lost my faith. I clung to it like a lifeline, knowing it was the only thing that could hold me together.

Not long after, I entered a marriage I thought would finally bring me stability. But faith can be weaponized, and that's what he did. He twisted scripture to justify his abuse, making me question myself, making me wonder if I was the problem. It was spiritual abuse, plain and simple.

The isolation, the manipulation, the relentless emotional warfare—it drained everything out of me. I began questioning my sanity. I remember lying in bed one night, staring at the ceiling, feeling like my mind was unraveling. I was in such a dark place that I didn't want to live anymore. It felt like the only escape from the torment was to give up. The weight of grief, trauma, and abuse collided all at once, leaving me mentally numb and emotionally paralyzed.

I knew I was fighting more than just a bad relationship—I was in a battle for my soul. Dark thoughts of suicide flooded my mind, and in that moment, I realized this wasn't just a physical or emotional fight anymore. I was facing a spiritual battle, an evil force that was trying to claim my life.

One Sunday, I dragged myself to church. At the end of the service, a sister came to me and said, "The Lord says, 'You shall leave, but not in haste or in flight.'" When I got home, I opened my Bible to Isaiah 52:11-12

"Depart, depart, go out from there! Touch no unclean thing! Come out from it and be pure, you who carry the articles of the Lord's house.

But you will not leave in haste or go in flight; for the Lord will go before you, the God of Israel will be your rear guard."

That promise became my anchor. I knew God was working out my departure.

The next week, Pastor Joe Johns began a series titled *"Coming Out of Your Egypt."* He spoke of the Israelites' journey—how God led them out of slavery, through the wilderness, and into the Promised Land. I sat there, barely breathing, as his words pierced my heart. He said, *"Everyone has an Egypt. It's that place where the Enemy is ruling over us, where we are slaves to fear and victims of our circumstances. It's the place where we feel lost and forgotten, where misery and struggle seem endless. Egypt is where we will perish if God doesn't rescue us. For some, Egypt is an addiction, mental health condition, or chronic sin. For others, it's the heartbreak of a lost dream, failed marriage, lost loved one, financial ruin, or a serious health event."*

I was in my own Egypt. I had been enslaved by trauma, by pain, by abuse—and God was calling me out. That moment was my turning point. I realized that if I stayed—if I allowed this man and these experiences to continue to break me—I was not just failing myself. I was failing the purpose God had for me. I had to leave. Not just for my sake, but for my grandkids, who were living with me at the time. I couldn't let them grow up in the toxic environment we were trapped in.

Leaving wasn't easy. I was judged by people I thought would support me. They quoted scripture about how *"God hates divorce"* and told me I should have fought harder for the marriage. But they didn't see what I saw. They didn't understand that staying in a toxic, abusive marriage was not God's will for me.

I had to walk away, even when it felt like the world was against me.

And that's when the women began to come forward.

One by one, women started confiding in me—women who were also trapped in abusive relationships with men who were supposed to be Christ followers. They spoke to me in whispers, afraid to be judged, afraid to leave—just as I had been.

But I saw their pain, and I understood it all too well.

That's when I realized what God had been preparing me for. Every trauma, every battle, every tear had been refining me for this ministry. I was meant to help these women. God didn't want me to stay in an abusive relationship—He wanted me to break free so I could help others find their freedom.

Through *2 Timothy 3*, I began to study how the Bible warns us about people with narcissistic qualities—those who are *"lovers of themselves, lovers of money, boastful, proud, abusive…"* These were the traits I had been living with. God's Word had already warned me, and now I was equipped to help other women see it too. I began to teach women that **God loves them more than He loves the institution of marriage.** The narrative that *"God hates divorce"* has been used to keep so many women trapped in abusive relationships. But I helped them understand this truth: they are the temple of the Holy Spirit. Their mind, body, and spirit are sacred, and God does not want them to endure self-abuse by allowing someone else to destroy them.

In the years since leaving that marriage, I have ministered to women who, like me, are navigating abusive relationships, trauma, and spiritual manipulation. These relationships are not limited to marriage—they can exist within families, workplaces, and friendships. I've seen firsthand the chains fall from women who thought they were alone, who believed they were trapped forever. And with every story I hear, with every woman I help, I'm reminded of God's purpose for me.

You see, what I've learned through all of this is that **trauma does not define us—it refines us.** God doesn't waste pain. He uses it to mold us, to strengthen us, to prepare us for the work He has called us to do. If I had stayed silent, if I had remained in my Egypt, I never would have found my calling.

To every woman who reads this, I want you to know: **You are not alone. You are not crazy. And God does not want you to remain in a place that destroys your spirit.** He loves you, and He has a purpose for you. Do not let guilt or fear hold you back from stepping into the life He has called you to. You are His temple, and it's time to protect that sacred space.

Let God lead you out of your Egypt. Trust Him to guide you into your promised land.

> *"I never imagined the moment that would break me*
> *would also be the one to set me free."*

Isaiah 52:11-12

"Depart ye, depart ye, go ye out from thence, touch no unclean *thing*; go ye out of the midst of her; be ye clean, that bear the vessels of the LORD. For ye shall not go out with haste, nor go by flight: for the LORD will go before you; and the God of Israel *will be* your rereward."

King James Version (KJV)

Chapter #39

MY FATHER'S DAUGHTER
Paige

Perception of identity. How others see you. How you see yourself. Who you want to be and what you want to be known for. So many factors shape our identities—our environment, whether we feel supported, whether we feel safe sharing pieces of ourselves. Some parts of our identity we proudly wear for the world to see. Others, we keep hidden, tucked away for ourselves or a lucky few. And then there are those who switch up their identities depending on who's around or who's paying attention. My father was the latter.

Anyone who had the pleasure of being in my father's company knows how charismatic and charming he could be. He was the life of the party, and he knew no stranger. As a child, I would get bored on errands because he'd stop to talk to *everyone*. I still hear his laughter—bellowing, booming across the room. Looking back, I realize now that much of his charm passed on to me. People saw him as this *"great"* guy—always friendly, always showing up for others. But he wasn't a great dad. When I needed him to be a father, he wasn't there.

My parents divorced when I was 10. I know this because my mother moved out just as I started fifth grade. It was the typical arrangement—living with Mom during the week and staying with Dad every other weekend. At first, it felt fine. I was even excited about having two bedrooms to decorate. But soon, the weekends became shorter and further apart until I lived with my mother full time.

I was a curious, driven child—always involved in school and my community. In high school, I was on the cheer squad, played softball, sang in choir and show choir, and excelled academically. My father came to only a handful of games or performances. Back then, it felt like I was never *enough*—never good enough, never important enough. His broken promises became a pattern. Something, or someone, always took precedence over me. I internalized that, believing I wasn't significant enough to deserve his time.

By college, communication with my father was scarce. I threw myself into school and my independence. My mother would call daily and ask, *"Have you talked to your dad?"* My answer was always the same: *"No."* When I did call him, it usually went to voicemail. Sometimes he called back, sometimes it was weeks before I'd hear from him. I'd hear through others that he was in my college town for events, yet he never called to meet up. Despite everything, I *desperately* wanted a connection with him.

Sports was our common ground—the one safe thing we could talk about. I fell in love with football because he took me to my first college game. My senior year of college, I invited him to "Senior Dad's Weekend," a lighthearted event where girls hang out with their dads and watch the game together. I gave him the date six months in advance and reminded him several times. He assured me he would come. Three weeks before the event, he told me he wasn't coming. I was heartbroken. I didn't even want to be on campus that weekend.

Eventually, I stopped expecting him to show up. I accepted that he didn't want to be a part of my life. By the time I graduated from grad school, it didn't even surprise me that he wasn't there.

When I moved home after school, we'd occasionally talk, but he felt more like a family acquaintance than a father. He'd invite me to dinner sometimes, or I'd text him during football games, but it was always surface level—sports and music, never life or feelings. I tried multiple times to tell him what I needed from him as my dad. I wrote letters, poured out my heart, and time after time, he would say, *"Things will be different."* For a week or two, they were. Then we'd settle back into the same painful cycle.

Years passed. I had my first "big girl" job, my own apartment, a new circle of friends, and a cat. Life was moving forward—until everything stopped.

I got the call right before leaving for vacation: *"Your father is in the hospital. He collapsed at work."* I visited him, and everything seemed fine. The doctors were still running tests. He told me to go on my trip, that he would call me with any updates.

Two days later, while sitting on an orange-cushioned bench in a dimly lit hotel lobby, I got the call that changed everything. Cancer. Not just cancer—stage IV. It started as colorectal cancer and spread to his liver. The words felt like a punch to the gut. I immediately blamed myself. *Why didn't I push him harder to get screened?* I had told my mother obsessively about screenings, but with my father, I let it slide.

The doctors told us it was terminal—he could slow it down but not beat it. Despite everything we had been through, I decided to be there for him. I threw myself into gathering resources, researching treatments, and asking questions, only to be met with vague answers. I felt shut out—insignificant. But I tried. I saw him often, and for a while, we got closer.

After two years of treatments, we ran out of options. He was tired, and his decline came quickly. As he lay in bed on hospice, I would sing to him. Singing had been our thing when I was little, and I'd have given anything to share one more song with him.

Toward the end, I searched my heart for forgiveness—for him not being the dad I needed, for the relationship I grieved but never truly had. I know he's no longer suffering, but I mourn the moments we'll never share. He won't walk me down the aisle. My future children will know him only through my stories. June, with Father's Day, his birthday, and the anniversary of his death, will always carry a sadness.

At this point in my life, I can recognize how my relationship with my father shaped me. I crave acceptance and struggle to trust, especially with men. It's something I work on every day. I've dedicated my career to helping families affected by cancer, honoring my father with every patient I'm privileged to support. I also want to be there for the children who experience the same loss I have.

Forgiveness is a choice—a conscious act to reclaim your power. When I think about forgiving my father, I remind myself that we are all doing the best we can with the cards we've been dealt. My father wasn't perfect. Neither am I. But I love him. I always will.

Through the pain, the love, and the loss, I will always be my father's daughter, and he will forever be a part of my identity.

Ephesians 4:31-32

"Let all bitterness, and wrath, and anger, and clamour, and evil speaking, be put away from you, with all malice. And be ye kind one to another, tenderhearted, forgiving one another, even as God for Christ's sake hath forgiven you."

King James Version (KJV)

Chapter #40

<u>LOSING MY AUNTS</u>
Nita

In the quiet of a twilight hour,
A whisper lingers, soft as flower,
Their echoes, a distant song,
In the heart where memories belong.

With every call, I felt their grace,
Their gentle smiles, their warm embrace,
They were aunts, yet more like sisters they gave me love and light,
Now shadows gather, dimming bright.

The world turned cold, a thief in the night,
Losing one aunt to kidney and heart failure and the other to COVID-
19,
these illnesses stole our delight,
They fought so bravely, with strength untold,
But fate seemed so cruel and bold.

I trace the lines of our shared days,
In the golden sun, in the softest haze,
Our stories danced like fireflies,
Now silence falls where laughter lies.

Though time may pass, and seasons change,
Aunt Vicki and Vanessa my heart hold you, though life feel strange,
In every tear, in every sigh,
Your spirits soar, they cannot die.

So here I stand missing you both in grief's embrace,
With memories of our conversations and laughter, a precious bond
that time cannot erase,
My dear aunts, more like sisters, and definitely my close friends,
In the tapestry of memory, you remain in my heart as it continues to
mend.

Isaiah 25:8

"He will swallow up death in victory; and the Lord GOD will wipe
away tears from off all faces; and the rebuke of his people shall he take
away from off all the earth: for the LORD hath spoken *it*."
King James Version (KJV)

Chapter #41

<u>**REVEALED**</u>
Evan

Uprooted, Restored, Revealed

Walking in purpose, silenced, *BE STILL.*
Exalted my thoughts and conscious way of being,
Stopped doubting, self-shaming—new horizons I'm seeing.

More than enough, sufficient, and polished,
May stumble here and there, but won't be demolished.
Growing in wisdom, knowledge, and understanding,
It's because of Allah, new seeds I'm constantly planting.

From You, through me, lives are being impacted,
Curses being broken, new ways of life spoken,
Blessings beyond wildest imagination,
Shedding old skin, embracing transformation.

He has not left me nor forsaken—
There were blessings in those storms,
Her-story in the making.

P-L-E-A-S-E be patient with me,
Still haven't come forth as pure gold.
In fact, far from being perfect,
But in His word, I stand and remain bold.

I hope these lines are sparking or rekindling your fire.
Don't give up, see your breakthrough, ignite that burning desire.

UNVEILED

You may be tired and ready to give in—
That's just the devil playing tricks,
Not wanting you to win.

In due time, my sister, it will be your season.
Stay ready, don't get ready—
You don't need any other reason.

The order of my steps is etched in righteousness.
It took the Almighty sending my soulmate to realize this.
My angel in disguise taught me how to persist;
Failures don't define, rather help you dismiss
All thoughts of doubt and unworthiness.

One foot in front of the other,
Can't keep looking behind—I've got to move forward.
Not dwelling in the past of chaos and disorder,
I'm trying to learn from the future on how to maneuver.

The workings of Allah have come in mysterious ways;
Many of them dark—then nights turned into days.
No better time than the present to embrace all He has in store.
Every time a window shut, He opened a BIGGER door.

Just like my momma and grand-momma's that came before,
Their spirits and prayers cover, *til this day,* help me endure.
In the lowest of my lows and highest of my highs,
All praises be to Thee—in Him my strength resides.

May He bless you and keep you,
Have faith, believe, and be healed.
Claim your victory, walk in purpose,
Be restored, and see the new you—
Revealed.

Galatians 6:9

"And let us not be weary in well doing: for in due season
we shall reap, if we faint not."
King James Version (KJV)

Chapter #42

FINDING MY PURPOSE THROUGH GRIEF

Dachele

June 3, 2024, was one of the worst days of my life. I lost my younger brother, Julius. I never thought I would live life without him. We shared forty-four years together—when you saw him, you saw me. My brother was spiritually driven. He taught me that no matter what life takes you through, always put God first. When I'm alone, I cry a lot and remember all of the good times we shared. It's not easy, but I know God makes no mistakes, and my brother's life was already written. God's plan was best for him. He allowed me forty-four years of experiencing a sibling's unconditional love and strong faith. Since my brother left this earth, I've learned to cherish every moment with family and love them as much as possible.

There have been moments when I felt weak, yet God showed me that I was strong, even through the pain in my heart. Now I understand that you don't "get over" grief, but there are ways to get through it. The first way I deal with grief is through prayer—understanding God's purpose and His plans for me. My next step is reading God's Word and allowing it to be a part of my daily life. My brother, being a spiritual person, taught me so much and helped me understand the Word. When I'm at church, I feel that our connection lives on through God's will. Each day, I live with the pain, but it will not break me—it will make me stronger because I serve an awesome God. He will see me through it all.

My advice to everyone reading this is to put God first—He will never fail you. God gives His toughest battles to His strongest soldiers, and I am on the battlefield for the Lord. Even though I'm dealing with the loss of my brother, I know in my heart he is no longer suffering. He is living in a palace far greater than earth. A word of advice from Psalm 30:5 says, *"Weeping may endure for a night, but joy comes in the morning."* Allow God to insert peace and joy into your life while you go through your healing process. If you don't attend church, make it a habit to receive God's Word. Why? Because God heals the brokenhearted. He will fix the broken pieces of your life, putting them together piece by piece.

God is our antidote to all situations. You must place Him in your heart and never give up. Better days will come if you trust Him, even while dealing with grief. If you allow God to work in your life, He will help you cope with the sadness and pain you feel. God can change your pain into purpose, equipping you to guide someone else who's going through the same situation. That's exactly what God is doing with me—according to His will. Even though I remain in deep thought about my brother's death and shed many tears, I pull myself together to motivate myself, live for God, and be there for my mother and the rest of my siblings.

God gives me strength every day to keep going and never give up. I draw inspiration from Job's story—when he felt he had lost everything, yet his faith in God remained strong. Job knew God's plan for his life was greater than his own, and he remained calm through the process. Isaiah 61 reminds us of God's promise to heal those who are sad and brokenhearted. Grief may bring those emotions, but God is our refuge. From this day forward, make God your priority, and He will change your life. Don't let grief break you—let it build you up.

My purpose is to help others find God and lead them to His Word. Without God, you'll feel lost trying to find your way. Hebrews 11:6 says, *"And without faith, it is impossible to please God because anyone who comes to Him must believe that He exists and that He rewards those who earnestly seek Him."* I've asked God to bless my purpose in life, but if my plan isn't what He desires, I ask Him to guide and redirect my path.

Trust in God's plan, seek Him daily, and let Him be the strength that carries you through every storm. He will never leave you.

Revelation 21:4

"And God shall wipe away all tears from their eyes; and there shall be no more death, neither sorrow, nor crying, neither shall there be any more pain: for the former things are passed away."
King James Version (KJV)

Chapter #43

<u>IN THE HOWLING AND PEACE</u>
Alysia

Each of us may have our way of sifting and shifting in the headwinds of trauma...
In the howling of the storm... in the breeze of peace...
I can only speak for my path, which may intersect with yours:

This is the part of trauma
Where the life I built is scattered and broken like gravel...
The presence of some loved ones, who joined as familiar building blocks of my regular or daily life,
Is suddenly and sharply smaller and smaller...
But God...
"[...] heals the brokenhearted and binds up their wounds" (Psalm 147:3, NKJV).

This is the part of trauma
Where others may throw stones at trauma with me
Or against my name as a survivor,

Making impact...
Someone speaks life to me from an unusual source or sight for sore eyes.
We push forward together against disturbances that engulf
But are not my entire being.
Another may knock me back through blowhard notions of misunderstanding...
In the media... on social media... at work...

Down the block... my family... in me... elsewhere...
The seen and unseen...
Never always knowing from where these gusts—back or ahead—may
come.

I seek the uplift of true wisdom,
And use my voice to edify and counter...
Keep going!
Thank you, Lord...
"[...] a refuge for the oppressed, a refuge in times of trouble" (Psalm
9:9, NKJV).

This is the part of trauma
Where I may see some repeats.
The winds of life encircle me...
With some lessons I may not have quite learned the first time...
Or, testimonies uniquely shaping me for ministry in connection.
In the howling... in the breeze of peace...
Anguish may continue... or return...
At times stacked.
And each load is eased by my healing journey,
So that the pain may constructively cease.

I am steady and ready...
In each season, I listen to how God guides.
Our Savior comforts...
"When you pass through the waters, I will be with you; and through
the rivers, they shall not overflow you. When you walk through the
fire, you shall not be burned, nor shall the flames scorch you" (Isaiah
43:2, NKJV).

In the howling... in the peace.

Psalms 9:9

"The LORD also will be a refuge for the oppressed, a refuge
in times of trouble."
King James Version (KJV)

Chapter #44

WILL IT EVER HAPPEN FOR ME?
Kela

July 13, 2002, was one of the happiest days of my life. As a matter of fact, that entire year was one to remember. I graduated with a Bachelor of Science degree in Psychological Science, moved to a new city, purchased my first home, started my first professional job, and married my college sweetheart. Whew... a lot happened in a short amount of time.

After about two months of marriage, I stopped taking birth control in hopes of one day conceiving a child. Over the years, my menstrual cycles became irregular, and I remembered my doctor's earlier warning that I might face issues trying to have children. At 22, I shrugged it off. I thought, *let me get this birth control out of my system, and everything will be fine*. But after a year and a half, I began to feel that something was wrong. My doctor diagnosed me with Polycystic Ovarian Syndrome (PCOS)—a hormonal imbalance that often causes reproductive challenges for women. PCOS led to weight gain, excess hair growth, and irregular ovulation, making it difficult to conceive naturally.

Some people think they have the right to pressure you into marriage and having children, but it didn't happen like that for me. I ended up seeing a fertility specialist. The medications I took made me feel horrible—physically and emotionally. If one dosage didn't work, the doctor increased it for the next cycle. The financial strain, emotional rollercoaster, and severe mood swings became unbearable. Clomid, in particular, made me feel *unhinged*! I didn't even recognize myself.

In 2005, I started graduate school, and having children was pushed to the back burner until 2008. That year, I was in my final year of graduate school and found out I was pregnant. I was overjoyed! I was due around Christmas, and I eagerly anticipated having a "Christmas baby." My husband and I were so excited—we told close friends and my in-laws.

But one day at work, I began to feel sick and went home. I noticed dried blood in my undergarments, which alarmed me. My doctor told me I was likely dehydrated and needed to rest. Weeks later, I went in for an appointment. The first visit, I heard my baby's heartbeat, but at the second appointment—when my husband was there—I didn't hear anything. The eerie silence in the room is something I'll never forget. My worst fear came true: I had miscarried.

I underwent a DNC procedure, and my grief process began. That loss shook me to my core, leading to an undiagnosed depression. The night before the procedure, I spoke to a young woman who shared her struggles with having an abortion. God anointed me to minister to her with love, accountability, comfort, and grace. In that moment, I forgot my own pain and disappointment because I was on assignment to model God's love.

But later that night, between 2:00 and 3:00 a.m., I woke up abruptly—screaming and hitting the wall. I can't recall if I was dreaming or what triggered me, but I was consumed by the realization: *I'm losing my child, yet someone else chose to terminate theirs.* It felt so unfair. I'm not passing judgment on anyone's choices, but at that moment, the pain was overwhelming.

To make matters worse, a family member told me, *"Your baby was probably a murderer, and God had to take the baby."* I was stunned. Although I knew it wasn't meant maliciously, it pierced my heart. I buried my shame and sadness, dodging conversations about children. I even told my husband at one point that he should divorce me and find someone who could give him children. That was one of the most foolish things I've ever said, but it's truly how I felt. My husband, however, stood by me and reassured me that my worth wasn't defined by my ability to have children.

Eventually, I sought counseling to process my grief. God began healing my heart, and over the years, the pain lessened. I never forgot my first child, Kameron. I don't know if Kameron was a boy or a girl, but I know my child is in paradise, worshiping the Lord.

Fast forward to 2014—I was pregnant again and ecstatic. I even bought a bag of candy to symbolize the "sweet news." But this time, I miscarried due to a condition called *Edwards Syndrome* or *Trisomy 18*. It's a rare genetic disorder causing abnormalities that often result in a short lifespan for the baby. My husband took this loss especially hard, and I found myself being strong for him.

The losses continued. By 2015, I had another pregnancy that ended quickly, so quickly that I delivered the baby at home. Blood was everywhere, and I was in excruciating pain. My husband, despite his weak stomach, refused to leave my side. In that moment, "for better or for worse" became very real for us.

At a follow-up appointment, my fertility doctor told me that if I didn't move forward with treatments, I could continue to miscarry. But I knew—I *knew*—that wasn't God's will for me.

In 2016, the Holy Spirit spoke to me: *"Recalibrate your faith."* My husband and I were instructed to take communion daily and thank God for our children. By December 2017, our first daughter was born— without any medical intervention. After 15 years of marriage, God gave us a miracle. That moment fulfilled Psalm 118:23 (KJV): *"This is the LORD's doing; it is marvelous in our eyes."*

In 2018 and 2020, God blessed us with two more daughters. Now, I have three children in heaven and three on earth.

Whether it's children or anything else, if God promises something, it *will* happen. But we must discern between God's promises and our own desires. Isaiah 55:11 (AMP) says: *"So shall My word be that goes forth out of My mouth: it shall not return to Me void [without producing any effect, useless], but it shall accomplish that which I please and purpose, and it shall prosper in the thing for which I sent it."*

God's Word doesn't return void. It goes out, fulfills its purpose, and prospers! I want to encourage anyone who's standing on a promise from God. It may not look like anything is happening, but God's ways are not ours. Sarah conceived at 90, and Abraham was 100—well beyond childbearing years—but God kept His promise.

There *was* heartache. There *was* shame. But there was also a Word from God that superseded everything else. My story is not just about finally becoming a mother at 37. It's about God using me to encourage others who are in their "meantime period"—the waiting season where God's promise hasn't yet manifested.

Grief and faith are not mutually exclusive. You can grieve and still trust God. The Church doesn't always teach us how to grieve properly while holding on to our faith. But questioning God doesn't mean we lack faith—it means we're human.

God planted a seed in me—not just to celebrate my miracles but to minister to others. Whether you're waiting on a business breakthrough, a spouse, household salvation, or deliverance, you may find yourself asking, *"Will it ever happen for me?"*

According to Ephesians 3:20 (AMP): *"Now to Him who is able to [carry out His purpose and] do superabundantly more than all that we dare ask or think [infinitely beyond our greatest prayers, hopes, or dreams], according to His power that is at work within us."*

Whatever "it" is for you—know this: If God has said it, it *will* happen. Ask me how I know.

Psalms 118:23

"This is the LORD'S doing; it *is* marvellous in our eyes."
King James Version (KJV)

Chapter #45

REBUILDING BRIDGES
Nita

Growing up, I often felt like a puzzle piece that didn't fit. If you've read Chapters 5, 10, 15, 20, 25, 30, 35, and 40, you've likely gathered that already. As you know, my grandparents raised me. They provided love and stability in a warm home, but it was a home that was fundamentally different.

My father, though physically present in my life, was emotionally distant. He seemed unsure of how to express affection. For years, I grappled with feelings of disconnection and confusion, often wondering why he didn't reach out more. As a child, I craved his validation and recognition—something I think is natural for any daughter to long for from her father. While my grandparents filled the emotional void with their unwavering support, wisdom, and kindness, a small part of me always ached for that father-daughter bond.

Fast forward to my late 40s—an age when I thought I was finally coming into my own. I had built a life filled with love, friendships, and personal growth, yet that lingering shadow of early disconnection remained. Then one unexpected day, my father called me. His voice trembled as he spoke, and I could hear the weight of his emotions. He was crying—asking for forgiveness—and in that moment, something shifted within me.

His vulnerability opened a door I thought had been locked shut forever. We began to talk more, sharing stories and slowly rebuilding a relationship that had been fractured for so long. It wasn't easy—years of silence and misunderstandings couldn't be erased overnight. Yet, with each conversation, I could feel the walls between us crumbling. We laughed. We cried. We navigated the complexities of our shared history together. My father was learning to express love in the ways I had always longed for, and I was learning to forgive and release the trauma I'd held onto for so long.

Just as we were beginning to forge a real connection, life threw us another curveball. My father was diagnosed with cancer. The news hit me like a freight train. After spending years longing for his presence in my life, the thought of losing him was unbearable. It stirred up an old ache—as if I were losing him all over again, just as I had in my childhood and teenage years.

In the days that followed, I found myself reflecting deeply on our journey. The laughter we shared, the stories we told, and the moments that finally brought us closer were now tinged with urgency. Yet, as I processed my emotions, I began to see the beauty in our struggle. Our relationship—while shadowed by years of disconnection—had also become a testament to resilience, healing, and the power of love.

As I write these words, my father is still battling cancer, and I pray that one day he will pick up this book and be proud of his oldest child. Together, we have learned to listen to each other's fears and hopes, forging a bond richer and deeper than I ever imagined possible. In this challenging time, I have found strength in our renewed relationship. My father may not have been the dad I envisioned as a child, but he is a man who is learning, who is trying, and who is willing to fight for our bond.

I've realized that love doesn't always come in the forms we expect. Sometimes, it's a soft whisper amidst the chaos—a quiet reassurance that we are still loved.

As I navigate this new reality, I hold on to hope. Hope that we can create more memories, that we can continue to learn from one another, and that we can cherish whatever time we have left. While the fear of losing him feels overwhelming, I also recognize that God has been with me every step of the way.

This journey with my father has taught me the beauty of resilience, forgiveness, and connection. No matter what lies ahead, I am grateful for the chance to truly know my father, to love him, and to be loved in return. In the face of uncertainty, our bond has become a beacon of light—a reminder that even broken relationships can be mended, and love can flourish when you put God at the center of it all.

2 Corinthians 5:18

"And all things *are* of God, who hath reconciled us to himself by Jesus Christ, and hath given to us the ministry of reconciliation;"
King James Version (KJV)

Chapter #46

<u>BEAUTY IS UGLY</u>
Natasha "Natty"

We want to be god/GOD.

We clamor for control—over things we did not create, over things like other people.
Their lives.
We have and give unwarranted opinions about their journeys, their decisions, their depression, their money problems, the way they should raise their children, their houses, their mishaps, mistakes, their joys, their successes, their education, their laughter, their sad faces, the way they should spend their money and their days.
They should go to church.
They should not stand for that.
They should not weep.
The way they think. The mud. The seep. The red eyes. No sleep.
They should not swallow pills to hide pain. They should not drink.
They should pay their bills on time.
Their relationships—
They are struggling.
They should not be this way. They should not like that. BE like that.
If only.
They didn't consider suicide.
They should not hide.

The way they worship. They should be themselves.
Beauty is first. Ugly.
god/GOD loves me?
They should not question.

THE MOST HIGH. Of all things.

This is not them.
They. Their/there.

This is us.
Me. Here.
I said: WE want to be god/GOD.
I meant: I want to be god/GOD.
I think.

They say: misery loves company.
This is why they—
I mean, ME—craves altar.

Maybe this is WHY?
They—
I mean, me—
has this incessant need to confess.
Maybe this IS why they—
I mean, me?—
plays slave to imagined obligation.
Goddaughter.

Can gawd (they. can't.) see me?
I.
Drown. Drink. Mend.
(Cannot mind) my own business.
Rather than look at them.
Than. See. Me.

I.
Battle. Scars. Stars. Galaxies.

Galatians 3:3. Ephemeral.
Ephesians 3:3.

I.
Revel. Reveal.
Revelations 5:5.

I am. No lion.
There is no food.

Only famine on my spinning/offering plates.

Who am I?
I am everything. But. god/GOD.
I am nothing. But. GOD/god.
I am unhinged.

I am glory.
Matthew 26:36-28. (Gethsemane) gate.

I swing.
Backwards/forwards.
Until I AM.
Undone. Unveiled.
Spirit dry. I cry feathers.

I become dust.
Desert myself to:
Living waters.
Transform. Transgress.
Swallow/overcome mountains.
Five stones at a desolate time.
To: 1st Samuel 17:40.
Myself.

My healing comes through asking. Seeking. Knocking.
Questioning. Wandering.
Beyond what I saw—
Was never taught.
Within the wilderness/holiness of myself.

Job 38:28: "Does the rain have a father?"
Seek ye first.
Faith is. Beyond.
Beauty . . .Everything.

Deuteronomy 32:2

"My doctrine shall drop as the rain, my speech shall distil as
the dew, as the small rain upon the tender herb, and as the
showers upon the grass:"
King James Version (KJV)

Chapter #47

<u>THE PILLAR WE ALL NEED</u>
Nita

For much of my life, I carried the weighty title of "the pillar" or "the rock" for my family and friends. It was a role I embraced with pride, believing that my strength could support those I loved during the toughest times. I was the one they turned to in moments of crisis, the one who offered a prayer, a listening ear, and a shoulder to lean on. But over time, the pressure of being the pillar began to take its toll. I often felt exhausted, overwhelmed, and, at times, utterly alone in my efforts.

It wasn't until a pivotal moment in my life that God revealed a profound truth to me: I am incapable of being that pillar on my own. While I had always believed that my strength came from within, I came to understand that true strength flows from a source far greater than myself—my Father, God.

As an African-American woman, I grew up celebrating self-sufficiency and independence. I was taught to be strong, to handle my problems, and to support others without appearing vulnerable. At the same time, I was raised to love, trust, and lean on God. Yet, a mindset of relentless independence can trick us into believing that we must bear our burdens alone. For a time, I fell into that trap. I thought that if I could just muster enough willpower or resilience, I could be the unwavering support that everyone needed.

But this belief was ultimately unsustainable. The more I tried to be that pillar, the more I felt the cracks beginning to show. I often found myself drained, struggling to summon the energy to help myself, let alone others. It was during these moments of weakness that God gently nudged me, reminding me that my strength is not my own.

In prayer and reflection, I began to realize the trauma I had inflicted upon myself by trying to rely solely on my own strength. I came to understand that God is the ultimate pillar—the foundation upon which everything stands. In my weakness, I discovered His strength. In my moments of doubt, I found reassurance. God revealed to me that I don't have to bear the weight of the world; I can fully and completely lean on Him.

This revelation was transformational. The pressure I had placed upon myself to take care of everything and everyone began to lift. I learned to invite God into my struggles, to share my burdens with Him, and to seek His guidance. Instead of trying to be a pillar of strength on my own, I began to see myself as a conduit of God's strength. When I feel weak, I turn to Him for the support I need, allowing His presence to fill me with the energy and courage to be there for others.

Embracing this new perspective has changed how I interact with my loved ones. I have learned to be honest about my struggles, sharing my vulnerabilities rather than hiding them. This openness has not only deepened my relationships, but also encouraged others to seek God's strength in their own lives. By acknowledging my limitations, I invite others to do the same.

Instead of feeling like I have to be the unwavering pillar, I have become a source of support rooted in faith. I can be strong for others, not because I have all the answers or the ability to carry them, but because I am connected to the ultimate source of strength—God.

The journey of recognizing God as the true pillar has been humbling and liberating. I have learned that it is okay to lean on Him and that my role is to reflect His strength to those around me. I am no longer striving to hold everything together on my own, for I know the One who holds all things together. And in that, I have found peace.

Psalms 18:2

"The LORD *is* my rock, and my fortress, and my deliverer; my God, my strength, in whom I will trust; my buckler, and the horn of my salvation, *and* my high tower."
King James Version (KJV)

Chapter #48

ASHES TO BEAUTY
Nita

WON'T HE DO IT! I have experienced my share of trauma—moments that challenged my spirit and tested my resilience. Yet, through it all, I discovered a profound truth: God has been my constant source of strength. I have faced trials—times when I thought I might not recover, when the shadows seemed too dark to navigate. But in those moments of despair, I found something incredible: the unwavering presence of God.

It's easy to question our faith during difficult times. I have grappled with doubt and fear, wondering why I had to endure such pain. Yet, as I sought solace in prayer and reflection, I began to see hope emerge. God was not only present in my suffering; He was actively working in my life, transforming my trauma into purpose. In the Bible, we are reminded that *"He will give beauty for ashes"* (Isaiah 61:3). This promise became my lifeline. I began to understand that my experiences, though painful, were not in vain. God was preparing me for something greater—a calling to minister to others who are hurting, to speak life into those who feel like giving up, to let my life witness to others who feel alone.

As I healed, I felt a deep desire to share pieces of my story. I wanted to give women a platform to share their stories so they could heal and help others do the same. God gave me the vision to write this book, *"UNVEILED: Overcoming Trauma to Walk in Your Divine Purpose."* I want others to know they are not alone in their struggles. God has taken my ashes and transformed them into a message of faith and resilience. I have witnessed the power of vulnerability—how sharing our struggles can create a safe space for others to open up and heal. It's a beautiful exchange: when we share our stories, we help lighten the load for one another.

Through it all, I have learned that God is faithful. He does not promise us a life free of pain or trauma, but He does promise to walk with us through it. In every moment of despair, I felt His presence guiding me, reminding me that my story is still being written. I encourage anyone who is going through trauma to hold on to hope. You may feel like you are standing in the ashes, but remember that beauty is on the horizon. God is working in ways you cannot yet see, and He is preparing you for a purpose beyond your imagination.

As I reflect on my journey, I am filled with gratitude. Every trial and moment of trauma has shaped me into the woman of God I am today—a resilient minister, educator, wife, mother, daughter, sister, and friend. I am a testament to the fact that God can take our deepest wounds and turn them into sources of strength and inspiration.

If you find yourself in a season of trauma, know this: you are not alone. Trust in God's faithfulness, lean into your healing, and watch as He transforms your ashes into beauty.

Isaiah 61:3

"To appoint unto them that mourn in Zion, to give unto them beauty for ashes, the oil of joy for mourning, the garment of praise for the spirit of heaviness; that they might be called trees of righteousness, the planting of the LORD, that he might be glorified."
King James Version (KJV)

Chapter #49

FIND STRENGTH
AND COMFORT IN FAITH

These women's excerpts, including my own, reveal a profound truth: trauma is a deeply distressing experience that can leave lasting scars on our mental, emotional, and physical well-being. Coping with trauma is not an easy road. It often requires both professional intervention and spiritual support. Amid this challenging journey, the teachings and wisdom of the Bible can serve as a wellspring of solace, guidance, and hope.

The Bible is a tapestry of stories about individuals who faced unimaginable adversity yet triumphed through their faith. Consider the story of Job—a man who endured devastating losses yet remained steadfast in his trust in God. Job's resilience, rooted in his unwavering faith, stands as a timeless reminder that even in our darkest moments, we can find strength by trusting in God's plan for us. Through faith, our tests can transform into our testimonies, and our messes can become powerful messages.

Scripture is rich with verses that bring comfort to those grappling with trauma. Psalm 23 is a familiar passage that offers reassurance of God's presence and protection during times of difficulty. The verse *"Even though I walk through the valley of the shadow of death, I will fear no evil, for you are with me"* speaks directly to the heart of anyone walking through pain, reminding us that God is always by our side, ready to comfort and guide us.

Perhaps the most challenging aspect of overcoming trauma is the act of forgiveness—letting go of the anger and pain caused by those who have hurt us. Forgiveness, central to the Bible's teachings, plays a critical role in healing. In Matthew 6:14-15, Jesus teaches, *"For if you forgive other people when they sin against you, your heavenly Father will also forgive you. But if you do not forgive others their sins, your Father will not forgive your sins."* This passage underscores the necessity of releasing resentment, as clinging to bitterness can hinder our healing. Forgiveness is not about condoning harm but about freeing ourselves from the chains of pain that hold us captive.

Romans 12:2 encourages believers to *"be transformed by the renewing of your mind."* This verse highlights the importance of fostering positive, edifying thoughts. Trauma can trap us in cycles of negative thinking—what I call "stinkin' thinkin'." The enemy wants us to dwell in bitterness and despair, but such thoughts can manifest as disease in our hearts and even lead to diseases in our bodies. Renewing the mind through scripture, prayer, and meditation helps us shift our perspective from despair to hope and healing.

Healing from trauma is not a quick fix; it is a journey that requires patience, self-compassion, and consistent effort. For some, the process may take months; for others, it may span years. The timeline is different for everyone, but the promise of God's healing is universal.

By praying, immersing ourselves in scripture, seeking God's comfort, practicing forgiveness, and continually renewing our minds, we open ourselves to the transformative power of faith. The road to healing is not easy, but with God's strength, we can find solace and hope as we navigate the challenges of overcoming trauma.

Trust that God is working in and through you, even in the midst of your pain. His Word is a light unto our path, illuminating the way forward. Let your faith be the anchor that holds you steady, and know that with Him, all things are possible.

Romans 12:2

"And be not conformed to this world: but be ye transformed by the renewing of your mind, that ye may prove what *is* that good, and acceptable, and perfect, will of God."
King James Version (KJV)

Chapter #50

<u>RISE UP</u>

We have allowed past traumas to rent space in our minds, hearts, and souls. As we heal, we begin to shed the layers of pain and fear that have held us captive, making space for growth and empowerment. With each step of healing, we open ourselves to all the wonderful blessings God has waiting for us. Yet, too often, we hold onto our hurts, our pains, and our trauma for far too long, leaving no room for His outpouring. It is time to let go and let God! Recognizing that healing is possible is the first vital step toward reclaiming our lives.

As women rise up, there is a growing emphasis on living authentically. Embracing who we are—our flaws, strengths, and everything in between—empowers us to step boldly into the fullness of our being. When we reject societal expectations and walk in alignment with our God-given purpose, we not only empower ourselves but also inspire those around us. Authenticity is the key to unlocking a life rooted in truth and purpose.

No woman should stand alone. The power of community in this journey cannot be overstated. Surrounding ourselves with supportive, like-minded women creates a nurturing environment where we can share our stories, lift one another up, and celebrate victories—whether big or small. Together, we can shatter the stigma surrounding trauma, normalizing the conversation around healing and empowerment.

Every woman carries within her a divine purpose, a calling deeply embedded in her soul. When we allow past traumas to dictate our lives, we often lose sight of that purpose. However, as we heal and rise, we begin to uncover our passions, dreams, and the unique callings placed upon us by God. Whether it's advocating for others, pursuing creative endeavors, stepping into leadership, or serving in ministry, embracing our divine purpose becomes an act of reclaiming what was once lost.

Walking in your divine purpose demands action. It requires us to release the past, set intentions, create goals, and take steps—no matter how small—toward the life God has planned for us. This might involve seeking new opportunities, challenging limiting beliefs, or making significant life changes. Remember, progress is progress, regardless of the pace. Each day, each step brings us closer to the life we are destined for.

As women continue to overcome trauma and walk in their divine purpose, we are rewriting the narrative of what it means to be a woman in today's world. Breaking free from the chains of the past is not easy, but it is both necessary and attainable. By prioritizing healing, embracing authenticity, fostering community, and stepping into our God-given purpose, we can not only transform our lives but also impact the world around us.

So, my sisters, let us rise together—not as individuals but as a unified force of strength, resilience, and hope. **IT'S TIME TO BREAK THE SILENCE!**

Romans 8:11

"But if the Spirit of him that raised up Jesus from the dead dwell in you, he that raised up Christ from the dead shall also quicken your mortal bodies by his Spirit that dwelleth in you."

King James Version (KJV)

Chapter #51

<u>EMBRACING YOUR WORTH</u>

In a world brimming with expectations, comparisons, and relentless pressures, it's easy for women to lose sight of their true worth and boundless potential. Society persistently bombards us with messages that whisper we are not thin enough, smart enough, successful enough, or simply *not enough*. But let me tell you this, loud and clear: **You are enough!** You are more than enough! You are uniquely beautiful, undeniably strong, infinitely capable, and created in the perfect image of God.

Believing in yourself is a powerful tool—a lifeline—that helps you navigate through life's trauma with grace, power, and confidence. It's about recognizing your own value, acknowledging your strengths, and embracing your flaws as part of what makes you beautifully and perfectly imperfect. When you begin to overcome trauma and truly believe in yourself, you open the door to endless possibilities and opportunities that align with your God-given desires and dreams.

Trauma has a way of whispering lies that strip us of our self-belief. But we must remind ourselves of *who we are* and *whose we are*. You are a child of the King, destined for greatness. Self-belief isn't about perfection or never stumbling. It's about trusting God and trusting yourself to handle whatever life may bring. It's about learning from the trauma, growing stronger with each setback, and rising with resilience and faith.

When you trust in God's plan, believe in your abilities, and listen to that still, small voice within, you empower yourself to take bold steps, pursue your passions, and create the life you were always meant to live. You become equipped not just to dream, but to make those dreams a reality.

Remember this: God and you are your biggest cheerleaders. Address your trauma head-on and celebrate every victory—no matter how small it may seem. Acknowledge your progress and the mountains you have climbed. Be kind to yourself. Practice self-care to nurture your mind, body, and soul. Surround yourself with people who lift you up, champion your goals, and remind you of your worth when you need it most.

Believe in your dreams. Believe in your power. Most importantly, believe in yourself. Whether or not you fully realize it yet, I am here to tell you: **You are a force to be reckoned with, a light that shines brightly in this world.** Embrace your uniqueness, your journey, and even your trauma. Yes, I said embrace your trauma—it has shaped you into the resilient, incredible woman you are today.

Stand tall. Speak your truth. Never, ever forget that you are enough, just as you are.

To every woman who has journeyed through this book, take a moment to reflect on how far you have come. You may have endured trials and trauma, but sister, you are still standing. Reflect on your strength, your beauty, and your worth. You are enough. You always have been, and you always will be.

Trust in yourself. Believe in yourself. And watch as God opens

doors you never imagined were possible. You are a masterpiece in the making—embrace it, own it, and let your light shine for all the world to see.

It is time for you to RISE UP and WALK IN YOUR DIVINE PURPOSE!

Romans 8:28

"And we know that all things work together for good to them that love God, to them who are the called according to *his* purpose."
King James Version (KJV)

JOURNAL ASSIGNMENT

Healing and moving forward from traumatic experiences is possible through faith in God, prayer, time, effort, and self-reflection. This journal assignment is designed to help you begin the process of overcoming trauma and stepping into your divine purpose. By exploring your experiences, thoughts, and feelings in a safe and supportive space, you will take the first steps toward healing, resilience, and transformation.

Instructions:

1. **Create a Safe Space:**
   Find a quiet and comfortable place where you can focus without distractions. This should be a space where you feel secure to reflect openly.

2. **Be Consistent:**
   Dedicate a specific time each day for journaling. Consistency is key to the healing process, and setting a routine can help you stay committed.

3. **Reflect on Your Trauma:**
   Identify a traumatic experience (or experiences) that has deeply impacted you. Write about how it has shaped your beliefs, behaviors—both negative and positive—and emotions.

4. **Detail Your Story:**
   Describe the specific details of the traumatic event(s) and how they've affected your life. Be honest and open as you explore these emotions. This is your safe space; let your truth flow.

5. **Assess Your Coping Mechanisms:**
   Reflect on how you have coped so far. Have you sought help

from a professional counselor, pastor, or trusted friends? Have you engaged in self-destructive behaviors, or have you tried to suppress your emotions?

6. **Evaluate the Impact on Relationships and Self-Worth:**
Think about how the trauma has influenced your relationships, self-esteem, and overall well-being. Has it affected how you see yourself and others?

7. **Challenge Negative Thought Patterns:**
Identify any negative beliefs that have emerged from the trauma. Write them down and actively challenge them. Replace them with positive affirmations and alternative perspectives rooted in truth and faith.

8. **Process Your Emotions:**
Explore the emotions tied to the traumatic event(s)—anger, sadness, guilt, shame, fear, or others. Allow yourself to feel these emotions without judgment.

9. **Develop Healthy Coping Mechanisms:**
Discover and practice positive coping strategies to manage your emotions and support your healing. Consider incorporating activities such as:

   o **Prayer and meditation**

   o **Daily journaling**

   o **Mindfulness exercises**

   o **Physical activity or exercise**

   o **Seeking support from a therapist, pastor, or support group**

10. **Set Goals for Healing:**
    Establish clear, actionable goals to nurture yourself, build resilience, and move forward in a positive direction. These goals can include small daily steps or long-term objectives to rebuild your life.

11. **Ask for Help:**
    True strength lies in seeking support when needed. Reach out to a counselor, therapist, pastor, or trusted individual. Never be ashamed to ask for help. Your well-being is worth the effort. Give yourself permission to prioritize YOU.

Final Thoughts:

Approach this assignment with self-compassion and kindness. Healing from trauma is a journey that takes time, patience, and prayer. Along the way, triggers may arise, but by leaning into faith, dedicating yourself to self-reflection, and surrounding yourself with supportive tools and people, you can begin to overcome the lasting effects of trauma.

Allow God's love to guide you through this process, and trust that brighter days are ahead. This is the beginning of a transformative chapter in your life—a step closer to embracing your divine purpose and living the abundant life God has planned for you.

Habakkuk 2:2

"And the LORD answered me, and said, Write the vision, and make *it* plain upon tables, that he may run that readeth it."
King James Version (KJV)

MY PRAYER FOR YOU

God, I come before You, lifting up every woman who carries the weight of past traumas, wounds that have left lasting marks on their hearts and minds. I pray for Your healing touch, Lord, to cover them completely, restoring their spirits and bringing them peace and wholeness.

May Your comforting presence surround every reader of this prayer. Guide them through the process of healing and renewal. Give them the strength to release the pain and sorrow that have weighed them down, replacing it with Your light, love, and unshakable hope. Grant them courage to face their past with honesty and vulnerability, trusting in the truth that You are with them every step of the way.

God, I ask for resilience to take root in their hearts. May they rise above their scars and struggles, emerging stronger, more resilient, and more grounded in their identity as Your beloved daughters. Remind them, Lord, that they are never alone. You are always near, ready to listen to their prayers, to comfort their weary hearts, and to infuse them with Your unending strength.

Bless them, Lord, with healing—not only for their minds but also for their bodies and spirits—so they may step boldly into lives of joy, purpose, and freedom. Break every chain that trauma has placed upon them, and guide them onto a path of restoration. Lead them into a future filled with Your grace, mercy, and divine promise.

May these women find hope in the knowledge that You are a God of redemption, a God who takes ashes and turns them into beauty. Fill them with the peace that surpasses all understanding, and let Your love be their foundation as they move forward.

In Your infinite wisdom and compassion, Lord, I trust You to bring healing and wholeness to all who are suffering. Let them feel Your presence in their lives and find strength in Your unwavering love.

Amen.

In Peace and Love,
Shenita "Nita" Bolton

Philippians 4:7

"And the peace of God, which passeth all understanding, shall keep your hearts and minds through Christ Jesus."
King James Version (KJV)

CONTRIBUTORS

Neco Beasley
Celestine (Johnson) Bireley
Shenita "Nita" Bolton
Rachel Bryant
Kizmet Byrd
Alysia (Hunt Williams) Calloway
Natasha Carrizosa/Natty Roots
Dachele Chambers
Lorna Clarke
Treva Datcher
Paige Edmonds
Cheri Gerzabek
Carol Gray-Greenway
Kela Guy
Jeanetta Harris
Dr. Wendy Hazel
Natisha Hilliard
Tamyra Kelly
Julie May
Janieka McCracken
Sireana Montalvo
Evan Parker-Davis
Niasha Piper
Ashley Scatena-Bond
Krissy Surface
Jacque Tate
Allison Washington-Lacey
Bridget Williams
Other Amazing Women Who Chose to Remain Anonymous

ABOUT THE AUTHOR

 Shenita "Nita" Bolton, Ed.S., is an author, educator, and minister whose life is a profound testament to resilience, faith, and self-discovery. Shenita has faced and overcome personal traumas with steadfast courage and an unshakable determination to heal and grow.

Drawing strength from prayer, gospel music, faith, and the practice of journaling, Shenita transformed her pain into purpose. Her journey of healing became a source of inspiration, empowering her to rise above adversity and fulfill her dreams. Shenita's life reflects the beauty of turning trials into triumphs and becoming a beacon of hope for others navigating similar challenges.

With a deep passion for positively impacting lives, Shenita shares her insights through writing, teaching, and ministering. Her words, rich with authenticity and empathy, resonate deeply, offering encouragement and guidance to those seeking healing and purpose.

Shenita "Nita" Bolton's debut book, *Unveiled: Overcoming Trauma to Walk in Your Divine Purpose*, stands as a powerful testament to the transformative power of faith, resilience, and introspection. Through her work, Shenita seeks to uplift and empower others to overcome their struggles, embrace their inner strength, and walk confidently in their divine purpose.

Matthew 11:28

"Come unto me, all *ye* that labour and are heavy laden, and I will give you rest."
King James Version (KJV)